Doing The Devil's Work Behind the Christian Mask

Behind the Mask, Volume 1

Ydna Serdna

Published by Writers Sidekick Publishing, 2024.

DOING THE DEVIL'S WORK BEHIND THE CHRISTIAN MASK

First edition. June 26, 2024.

Copyright © 2024 Ydna Serdna.

ISBN: 979-8227771681

Written by Ydna Serdna.

Preface

There is a contradiction between the core teachings of Christianity and the actions of some who profess to follow it. When read with a genuine desire to understand and embody its teachings, the Bible promotes love, acceptance, and humility. Yet, instead of reflecting these values, some hide behind a facade of righteousness to justify their misdeeds and project their sins onto others.

It's puzzling and disheartening that people can read the same scriptures. Yet, some emerge with love messages and others with hate messages. This discrepancy often arises from a shallow or misguided interpretation of the Bible, influenced more by personal biases and societal pressures than by a proper understanding of the text. True Christianity, at its core, is about loving others as oneself, showing compassion, and refraining from judgment. When people use their faith to justify harmful behavior, they stray far from these principles.

The LARK Code—love, accept, respect, and know yourself—captures the essence of living a life in harmony with Christian values. When individuals genuinely embrace these principles, they enhance their lives and contribute to a more compassionate and understanding society. Self-love and self-awareness are fundamental to extending love and acceptance to others.

The tendency to judge others harshly often stems from a lack of self-love and an unwillingness to confront one's flaws. It's easier to point fingers than to look inward and address personal shortcomings. This behavior is antithetical to the teachings of Christ, who emphasized forgiveness, understanding, and humility.

Quoting the Bible should come from sincere understanding and reflection, not hearsay or a desire to manipulate others. Attending church should be about community, worship, and spiritual growth, not gossip or maintaining a false image.

Incidents of hate, discrimination, and other sins committed under the guise of Christianity are a betrayal of the faith's valid message. If more people embraced the true spirit of Christianity—marked by love, acceptance, and self-awareness—the world, indeed, would be a better place.

So, the challenge remains: to live authentically, to love oneself and others, and to embody the actual teachings of Christianity. Doing so can create a more inclusive, compassionate, and understanding world.

What Are Christianity's Values

Christianity, at its core, offers a rich tapestry of values that shape the lives of its adherents. Here are some of the fundamental values:

Love: The Cornerstone Of Christianity

In Christianity, love isn't just a feeling; it's a profound, transformative force that shapes every aspect of a believer's life. Jesus places love at the center of his teachings, highlighting its unparalleled importance.

Jesus's Teachings on Love

Jesus encapsulates the essence of love in the Great Commandment: "Love the Lord your God with all your heart and with all your soul and with all your mind and with all your strength. The second is this: 'Love your neighbor as yourself.' There is no commandment greater than these" (Mark 12:30-31). This commandment emphasizes the love for God and stresses the importance of loving others.

Loving Your Neighbor

To love your neighbor as yourself means treating others with the same care and consideration you would want for yourself. This kind of love is active, requiring more than just good intentions. It involves:

Acts of Kindness: Small, everyday actions demonstrating care and concern, like helping a friend in need or offering a kind word to a stranger.

Compassion: Feeling and expressing deep sympathy and concern for the suffering of others and being motivated to help.

Empathy: Understanding and sharing the feelings of others, putting oneself in their shoes to truly appreciate their experiences and emotions.

Loving Your Enemies

One of the most radical aspects of Jesus's teachings is the call to love one's enemies. In the Sermon on the Mount, Jesus states, "But I tell you, love your enemies and pray for those who persecute you" (Matthew 5:44). This instruction challenges believers to transcend natural inclinations of revenge and hatred, promoting:

Forgiveness: Letting go of grudges and anger and offering pardon to those who have wronged you.

Prayer: Actively praying for the well-being and transformation of those who oppose you.

Understanding: Seeking to understand the perspectives and motivations of your adversaries, fostering a spirit of reconciliation rather than conflict.

Selfless Acts of Love

Christian love is marked by selflessness, where one's actions are motivated by the well-being of others rather than personal gain. This selflessness mirrors the ultimate act of love demonstrated - by Jesus himself - his sacrifice on the cross for the salvation of humanity. Believers are called to:

Serve Others: Following Jesus's example of servanthood, believers are encouraged to serve those around them humbly and without expectation of reward.

Sacrifice: Sometimes, love requires personal sacrifice, whether it's time, resources, or personal comfort, for the benefit of others.

The Transformative Power of Love

When practiced genuinely, love has the power to transform lives and communities. It breaks d barriers, heals wounds, and fosters a sense of unity and peace. The early Christian community is a testament to this, as they were known for their love and support for one another, which attracted many to the faith.

In essence, love is the bedrock upon which Christianity is built. It's a dynamic, active force that calls believers to rise above selfishness, embrace empathy, and cultivate genuine care for all, including those who may be most challenging to love. By embodying this love, Christians aim to reflect God's love to the world, creating a ripple effect of kindness, compassion, and understanding.

Forgiveness: A Central Value In Christianity

Forgiveness lies at the heart of Christian teachings, emphasizing the necessity of releasing grudges and extending second chances. It is a powerful act reflecting God's mercy and grace, inviting believers to embody these qualities.

Biblical Foundations of Forgiveness

The Bible is replete with teachings on forgiveness, starting from the Old Testament and culminating in the New Testament with the life and teachings of Jesus Christ. One of the most prominent references is the Lord's Prayer, which millions of Christians recite daily: "Forgive us our debts, as we also have forgiven our debtors" (Matthew 6:12). This prayer underscores two critical aspects of forgiveness:

Seeking Forgiveness from God: Recognizing human imperfection and the need for divine mercy.

Extending Forgiveness to Others: Committing to forgive those who have wronged us reflects the forgiveness we receive from God.

The Example of Jesus

Jesus's life and teachings provide the ultimate model of forgiveness. On the cross, facing immense suffering, Jesus prays for his persecutors, saying, "Father, forgive them, for they do not know what they are doing" (Luke 23:34). This profound act of forgiveness illustrates several fundamental principles:

Unconditional Forgiveness: Forgiving without waiting for an apology or change in the other person.

Compassion: Understanding the humanity and frailty of others, which leads to mercy rather than judgment.

Redemption: Offering the possibility of a new beginning, even to those who seem undeserving.

The Power of Letting Go

Forgiveness is not just about absolving others but also about personal liberation. Holding onto grudges and resentment can weigh heavily on one's heart and mind. By forgiving, individuals can:

Find Peace: Releasing anger and bitterness can lead to inner peace and emotional healing.

Restore Relationships: Forgiveness can mend broken relationships, fostering reconciliation and deeper connections.

Reflect God's Love: Forgiving others is a way to mirror God's infinite love and mercy, demonstrating the transformative power of grace.

Practical Steps to Forgive

Forgiveness can be challenging, especially when dealing with deep hurts. However, Christianity offers practical guidance to help believers on this path:

Prayer: Praying for the strength to forgive and the well-being of those who have caused harm.

Reflection: Contemplating Jesus's teachings and his example of forgiveness can inspire and strengthen one's resolve.

Empathy: Trying to understand the perspective and circumstances of the wrongdoer can foster compassion and facilitate forgiveness.

Action: Taking concrete steps, such as reaching out to the person or letting go of negative thoughts, can help forgive.

The Commitment to Forgive

Forgiveness is not a one-time act but a continual practice. It requires a commitment to forgive repeatedly, as emphasized by Jesus when he tells Peter to forgive "not seven times, but seventy-seven times" (Matthew 18:22). This signifies an ongoing attitude of forgiveness, where believers are encouraged to:

Be Patient: Understanding that forgiveness can take time and must be revisited.

Stay Open: Remaining open to reconciliation and healing, even if it takes repeated efforts.

Forgiveness in Community

Forgiveness also plays a vital role in the life of the Christian community. The early church was built on mutual support, accountability, and forgiveness. In his letters, Paul urges believers to "bear with each other and forgive one another if any of you has a grievance against someone. Forgive as the Lord forgave you" (Colossians 3:13). This communal aspect of forgiveness fosters a culture of grace and understanding, essential for the health and unity of the church.

In summary, forgiveness in Christianity is a profound, multi-faceted value that embodies the essence of God's mercy. It calls believers to release grudges, offer second chances, and reflect divine grace in their interactions. By practicing forgiveness, Christians experience personal liberation and contribute to a more compassionate and harmonious world.

Humility: A Key Virtue In Christianity

Humility holds a place of great importance in Christian teachings. It values others above oneself and recognizes one's limitations and need for God's guidance. Jesus Christ is the ultimate exemplar of humility through his actions, teachings, and sacrifice.

Jesus as the Model of Humility

Jesus's life is a testament to humility. From his birth in a lowly manger to his death on the cross, he embodies humility in every aspect. One of the most striking examples is the washing of his disciples' feet:

Service to Others: In John 13:1-17, Jesus, the Son of God, takes on the role of a servant, washing the feet of his disciples. This act of service highlights the importance of humility and serving others, regardless of status or position.

Teaching by Example: Jesus explicitly tells his disciples, "I have set you an example that you should do as I have done for you" (John 13:15). He encourages them to practice humility by serving each other.

Teachings on Humility

Jesus frequently teaches about humility, emphasizing that it is fundamental to living a righteous life. One of his notable teachings is in Matthew 23:12, where he says, "For those who exalt themselves will be humbled, and those who humble themselves will be exalted." This reflects the divine principle that true greatness comes from humility:

The Beatitudes: In the Sermon on the Mount, Jesus blesses the "poor in spirit," acknowledging those who recognize their spiritual neediness and dependence on God (Matthew 5:3).

The Greatest in the Kingdom: Jesus explains that "the greatest among you will be your servant" (Matthew 23:11). This reverses societal norms, placing humility and service above power and pride.

Living Out Humility

Christians are called to live out humility in their daily lives. This involves several practical steps:

Self-awareness: Acknowledging one's flaws and limitations and being open to correction and growth.

Valuing Others: Philippians 2:3-4 advises believers to "do nothing out of selfish ambition or vain conceit. Rather, in humility, value others above yourselves, not looking to your interests but each of you to the interests of the others."

Serving: Following Jesus's example by actively seeking opportunities to serve others, especially those marginalized or in need.

The Paradox of Humility

Jesus often speaks in paradoxes to highlight spiritual truths. One such paradox is found in Matthew 19:30: "But many who are first will be last, and many who are last will be first." This teaches that true honor and reward in God's kingdom come from humble service and selflessness rather than seeking power and recognition.

Humility in Relationships

Humility profoundly impacts relationships, fostering peace and unity. It helps in:

Resolving Conflicts: A humble attitude allows individuals to listen, apologize, and reconcile rather than insisting on being right or holding grudges.

Building Community: In a community where members practice humility, there is mutual respect, support, and a willingness to serve one another, reflecting the body of Christ.

Humility Before God

Humility is also about recognizing one's dependence on God. James 4:10 urges believers to "humble yourselves before the Lord, and he will lift you up." This means acknowledging that all gifts and successes come from God and submitting to His will.

The Reward of Humility

The Bible promises humility leads to exaltation and honor in God's eyes. Proverbs 22:4 states, "Humility is the fear of the Lord; its wages are riches and honor and life." While the world may not always value humility, God sees and rewards the humble heart.

In essence, humility in Christianity is about a deep understanding of one's position in relation to God and others. It involves a willingness to serve, to place others above oneself, and to seek God's guidance in all things. By embracing humility, Christians aim to reflect the character of Christ, building a community grounded in love, service, and mutual respect.

Grace: The Unearned Favor Of God

Grace is a cornerstone in Christian theology, embodying that God's favor, blessings, and salvation are granted freely and not earned by human effort. It is a profound expression of God's love and mercy, offering believers a foundation of hope and assurance.

Understanding Grace

Grace is often defined as the unmerited favor of God. It means receiving good from God that we do not deserve and cannot earn through our actions. This concept is vividly illustrated in the New Testament, particularly in the writings of the Apostle Paul.

Biblical Foundations of Grace

The Bible provides numerous references to grace, emphasizing its pivotal role in the Christian faith:

Ephesians 2:8-9: "For it is by grace you have been saved, through faith—and this is not from yourselves, it is the gift of God—not by works so that no one can boast." This passage underscores that salvation is a gift from God, not a result of human effort or merit.

Romans 3:23-24: "For all have sinned and fall short of the glory of God, and all are justified freely by his grace through the redemption that came by Christ Jesus." This highlights that despite human sinfulness, grace brings justification and redemption.

Grace in Salvation

Grace is central to the Christian understanding of salvation. According to Christian belief, humanity is inherently sinful and separated from God. No amount of good deeds can bridge this gap. However, through Jesus Christ's sacrificial death and resurrection, God extends grace to humanity:

Atonement: Jesus's death on the cross atones human sin, satisfying the demands of justice while offering mercy. This act of grace provides the means for reconciliation with God.

Faith: Receiving this grace requires faith, which is seen as a gift from God. Believers trust Jesus's finished work on the cross rather than their efforts.

Grace in Daily Life

Grace isn't limited to the moment of salvation; it permeates every aspect of a Christian's life:

Sustaining Grace: God's grace strengthens and supports daily challenges and spiritual growth. Paul writes in 2 Corinthians 12:9, "My grace is sufficient for you, for my power is made perfect in weakness." This means that God's grace empowers believers to persevere and grow despite their weaknesses.

Transforming Grace: Grace also transforms believers, enabling them to live in a way that reflects God's love and holiness. Titus 2:11-12 states, "For the grace of God has appeared that offers salvation to all people. It teaches us to say 'No' to ungodliness and worldly passions and to live self-controlled, upright, and godly lives."

Grace and Good Works

While grace means that works do not earn salvation, it does lead to good works as a natural response to God's love:

Response to Grace: A genuine experience of God's grace inspires believers to live lives of gratitude and service. Ephesians 2:10 explains, "For we are God's handiwork, created in Christ Jesus to do good works, which God prepared in advance for us to do."

Fruit of the Spirit: Grace produces the fruit of the Spirit—love, joy, peace, patience, kindness, goodness, faithfulness, gentleness, and self-control (Galatians 5:22-23)—in the lives of believers, reflecting God's character.

Grace in Relationships

Grace also shapes how Christians interact with others:

Forgiveness: Just as they have received grace and forgiveness from God, Christians are called to extend grace to others, forgiving as they have been forgiven (Colossians 3:13).

Charity: Grace leads to acts of charity and compassion, helping those in need without expecting anything in return. It's about reflecting God's unconditional love.

Grace as a Source of Assurance

Grace provides believers with assurance and security in their relationship with God:

Eternal Security: Knowing that salvation is based on God's grace and not human performance gives believers confidence in their eternal destiny.

Freedom from Fear: Grace dispels fear of judgment and punishment, fostering a relationship with God based on love and trust.

Living in Grace

Living in grace means continually relying on God's unmerited favor and allowing it to shape one's life and actions:

Dependence on God: Recognizing that all strength, wisdom, and provision come from God.

Humility: Understanding that all achievements and blessings are gifts of grace, leading to a humble and thankful heart.

In summary, grace in Christianity is God's undeserved kindness and mercy, which are foundational to salvation and the Christian life. It teaches that all blessings, including salvation, come not from human effort but from God's immense love. By embracing grace, believers find strength, transformation, and the ability to extend God's love to others.

Compassion: A Core Christian Value

Compassion is a fundamental Christian value, inspiring believers to care for the sick, the poor, and the marginalized. It embodies a deep sense of empathy and a commitment to alleviate suffering, reflecting the heart of Jesus's teachings and actions.

Biblical Foundations of Compassion

The Bible is rich with exhortations and examples of compassion:

Old Testament: The Old Testament frequently commands care for the vulnerable. For instance, Deuteronomy 15:11 states, "For there will never cease to be poor in the land. Therefore I command you, 'You shall open wide your hand to your brother, to the needy and to the poor, in your land.'"

New Testament: Jesus emphasizes compassion throughout his ministry, demonstrating it through his miracles and teachings. One prominent example is Matthew 9:36, where Jesus, seeing the crowds, "had compassion on them, because they were harassed and helpless, like sheep without a shepherd."

The Parable of the Good Samaritan

One of Jesus's most powerful teachings on compassion is the Parable of the Good Samaritan (Luke 10:25-37):

The Story: In this parable, a man is beaten and left for dead on the road. A priest and a Levite, both respected figures, pass by without helping. A Samaritan considered an outcast by Jewish society, stops and tends to the man's wounds, takes him to an inn, and pays for his care.

The Lesson: Jesus uses this parable to redefine the concept of "neighbor" and to emphasize that genuine compassion transcends social and ethnic boundaries. The Samaritan's actions exemplify mercy and love, showing that compassion involves feelings and concrete acts of kindness.

Jesus's Ministry of Compassion

Throughout his ministry, Jesus consistently demonstrates compassion:

Healing the Sick: Jesus heals many, including lepers, the blind, and the paralyzed, showing that compassion involves addressing physical suffering (Matthew 14:14).

Feeding the Hungry: Jesus feeds large crowds, such as feeding the 5,000, showing that compassion also addresses basic human needs (Matthew 15:32-38).

Comforting the Mourning: Jesus weeps with those who mourn, such as at the death of Lazarus, showing empathy and emotional support (John 11:35).

Compassion in Christian Life

Christians are called to emulate Jesus's compassion in their daily lives:

Caring for the Sick: Visiting and caring for the ill within the community and broader society is a practical expression of compassion.

Helping the Poor: Christians are urged to assist those in financial need through charitable giving, supporting social justice initiatives, and providing practical help.

Supporting the Marginalized: Advocacy and support for marginalized groups, such as immigrants, prisoners, and those facing discrimination, reflect a commitment to justice and mercy.

Practical Steps to Show Compassion

Living out compassion requires intentionality and action:

Listening: Compassion starts with listening to the struggles and stories of others without judgment.

Acts of Service: Volunteering time and resources to help those in need, whether through local charities, church programs, or individual efforts.

Advocacy: Speaking up for those who cannot speak for themselves, engaging in efforts to bring about systemic change to alleviate suffering.

The Role of the Church in Compassion

The church plays a crucial role in fostering and facilitating acts of compassion:

Community Outreach: Many churches run programs such as food banks, homeless shelters, and medical clinics to serve their communities.

Global Missions: Churches often support international missions that provide healthcare, education, and economic support in developing countries.

Disaster Relief: Christian organizations frequently participate in disaster relief efforts, providing immediate and long-term assistance to those affected by natural disasters.

The Transformative Power of Compassion

Compassion has the power to transform both the giver and the receiver:

For the Receiver: Acts of compassion can provide physical relief, emotional support, and a sense of dignity and worth.

For the Giver: Practicing compassion fosters empathy, humility, and a deeper understanding of God's love, leading to personal spiritual growth.

Compassion as a Reflection of God's Love

Ultimately, compassion is a reflection of God's love for humanity:

Divine Example: God's compassion is evident in His patience and mercy towards humankind, providing salvation and comfort through Jesus Christ.

Imitation of Christ: By showing compassion, Christians imitate Christ and bear witness to His love tangibly.

In summary, compassion in Christianity is about more than feeling sympathy; it involves active, selfless efforts to alleviate the suffering of others. Through biblical teachings, Jesus's example, and practical application, Christians are called to embody compassion, making a positive and transformative impact on the world around them.

Justice: A Call For Fair And Equitable Treatment In

Christianity

Justice is a core value in Christianity, emphasizing the need for fair and equitable treatment of all people. This commitment to justice involves standing against oppression, advocating for the rights of the vulnerable, and promoting righteousness in society.

Biblical Foundations of Justice

The Bible strongly emphasizes justice, presenting it as a critical attribute of God and a fundamental expectation for His followers:

Old Testament: The Hebrew word for justice, "mishpat," appears frequently, underscoring God's concern for fairness and righteousness. For example, Micah 6:8 states, "He has sh you, O mortal, what is good. And what does the Lord require of you? Act justly, love mercy, and walk humbly with your God."

New Testament: Jesus continues this emphasis, advocating for justice in his teachings and actions. In Matthew 23:23, he criticizes religious leaders for neglecting "the more important matters of the law—justice, mercy, and faithfulness."

Jesus's Teachings on Justice

Jesus's ministry is a powerful testament to the importance of justice:

The Beatitudes: In the Sermon on the Mount, Jesus blesses those who "hunger and thirst for righteousness" (Matthew 5:6), highlighting the desire for justice as a virtue.

Parables: Through parables like the Sheep and the Goats (Matthew 25:31-46), Jesus emphasizes caring for the marginalized, equating such actions with service to him.

Justice in Action: Advocating for the Vulnerable

Christianity calls for active engagement in promoting justice, particularly for the vulnerable:

Defending the Oppressed: Isaiah 1:17 commands, "Learn to do right; seek justice. Defend the oppressed. Take up the fatherless's cause; plead the widow's case." This highlights a proactive stance in defending those who are marginalized.

Speaking Against Injustice: Proverbs 31:8-9 urges believers to "Speak up for those who cannot speak for themselves, for the rights of all destitute. Speak up and judge fairly; defend the rights of the poor and needy."

Practical Steps for Pursuing Justice

Christians are encouraged to take practical steps in their pursuit of justice:

Awareness and Education: The first step is to understand the issues of injustice locally and globally. This includes learning about systemic inequalities, human rights abuses, and social injustices.

Advocacy and Activism: Christians can advocate for justice through peaceful protests, writing to legislators, and supporting policies that promote fairness and equality.

Charitable Work: Engaging in or supporting organizations that alleviate poverty, provide legal aid, and support victims of injustice.

Personal Conduct: Living out justice in daily interactions by treating others fairly, respecting their rights, and challenging unjust practices in one's community.

Justice in the Church

The church has a significant role in promoting justice:

Community Support: Many churches run programs to support the needy, such as food banks, shelters, and legal aid services.

Educational Initiatives: Churches often educate their members about social justice issues and biblical perspectives on justice.

Mission Work: Engaging in mission work to improve living conditions, provide education, and advocate for human rights worldwide.

Historical Examples of Christian Justice

Throughout history, many Christians have made significant contributions to justice:

Abolition of Slavery: Christian leaders like William Wilberforce in the UK and Harriet Tubman in the US played pivotal roles in the abolition of slavery.

Civil Rights Movement: Figures like Martin Luther King Jr. drew on their Christian faith to advocate for civil rights and racial equality.

Social Reforms: Many Christians have been involved in movements for workers' rights, women's suffrage, and child labor laws.

Theological Foundations of Justice

Justice is deeply rooted in the nature of God:

God's Justice: The Bible portrays God as a just judge who cares for the oppressed and demands righteousness (Psalm 103:6, Deuteronomy 32:4).

Imago Dei: The belief that all humans are created in the image of God (Genesis 1:27) underpins the call for equal treatment and respect for all people.

Challenges in Pursuing Justice

Pursuing justice can be challenging and requires perseverance:

Opposition and Persecution: Those who stand up for justice often face resistance, hostility, and even persecution.

Complexity of Issues: Social justice issues are often complex and multifaceted, requiring careful and sustained efforts to address them.

Justice and Mercy

Justice in Christianity is balanced with mercy:

Micah 6:8: The call to "act justly and to love mercy" reflects the need to pursue justice with a heart of compassion and kindness.

Jesus's Example: Jesus embodies justice and mercy, offering forgiveness and advocating for the oppressed.

In summary, justice in Christianity is about ensuring fair and equitable treatment for all, standing up against oppression, and advocating for the rights of the vulnerable. Grounded in biblical teachings and exemplified by Jesus, this pursuit of justice calls for active engagement, personal integrity, and a commitment to transforming society according to the principles of righteousness and compassion.

Faith: The Bedrock Of A Christian's Relationship With

God

Faith is central to Christianity, the foundation of a believer's relationship with God. It is characterized by trust and belief in God's promises, even without physical evidence. The essence of faith is succinctly captured in Hebrews 11:1: "Now faith is confidence in what we hope for and assurance about what we do not see."

Biblical Definition of Faith

The Bible provides a clear and comprehensive understanding of faith:

Hebrews 11:1: This verse defines faith as having confidence in what we hope for and assurance about what we do not see. It underscores the belief in the unseen and the future fulfillment of God's promises.

Examples in Scripture: Hebrews 11, often referred to as the "Faith Chapter," lists numerous examples of individuals who demonstrated faith in God's promises despite not seeing them fulfilled in their lifetimes.

Components of Faith

Faith in Christianity encompasses several key components:

Belief in God: Faith begins with a belief in the existence of God and His nature as revealed in the Bible. This includes belief in His goodness, sovereignty, and love.

Trust in God's Promises: Faith involves trusting that God will fulfill His promises, even when circumstances suggest otherwise. This trust is based on God's character and past faithfulness.

Obedience: Genuine faith leads to obedience. Believers act according to God's commands, trusting His ways are best.

Hope: Faith is closely linked with hope, the confident expectation that God will bring about His purposes and that there is a future reality aligned with His promises.

Faith in Action

Faith is not just an intellectual assent but is demonstrated through actions:

Abraham: Kn as the "father of faith," Abraham left his homeland and was willing to sacrifice his son, Isaac, demonstrating his trust in God's promises (Hebrews 11:8-19).

Moses: By faith, Moses led the Israelites out of Egypt, trusting God's deliverance and guidance (Hebrews 11:23-29).

Everyday Believers: Christians today live out their faith through acts of service, worship, and adherence to God's commands, trusting in His guidance and provision.

Faith and Salvation

Faith is fundamental to the Christian understanding of salvation:

Ephesians 2:8-9: "For it is by grace you have been saved, through faith—and this is not from yourselves, it is the gift of God—not by works so that no one can boast." This passage highlights that salvation is a gift received through faith, not earned by works.

Justification by Faith: Romans 5:1 states, "Therefore, since we have been justified through faith, we have peace with God through our Lord Jesus Christ." Justification, declared righteous before God, comes through faith in Jesus Christ.

Faith in Daily Life

Faith impacts every aspect of a Christian's daily life:

Decision Making: Believers make decisions based on their trust in God's wisdom and guidance, seeking His will through prayer and Scripture.

Facing Trials: Faith provides strength and comfort in difficult times. James 1:2-3 encourages believers to consider trials as opportunities to grow in faith.

Relationships: Faith shapes how Christians interact with others, promoting love, forgiveness, and humility.

Growing in Faith

Faith is dynamic and can grow over time through various means:

Prayer: Regular communication with God strengthens trust and reliance on Him.

Scripture: Studying the Bible deepens understanding of God's promises and His faithfulness throughout history.

Community: Fellowship with other believers provides support, encouragement, and opportunities to witness faith in action.

Challenges to Faith

Christians may face challenges that test their faith:

Doubt: Periods of doubt are natural and can lead to a deeper, more resilient faith when addressed through prayer, study, and counsel.

Suffering: Difficult circumstances can challenge faith but provide opportunities to trust God more deeply and experience His comfort and strength.

Faith and Reason

Christian faith is not blind but is supported by reason and evidence:

Historical Evidence: The historical reliability of the Bible, the life and resurrection of Jesus, and the testimony of early Christians provide a foundation for faith.

Personal Experience: Believers often cite personal experiences of God's presence, guidance, and answered prayers as evidence of their faith.

In summary, faith in Christianity is a profound trust and belief in God and His promises, even without physical proof. It encompasses belief, trust, obedience, and hope, shaping every aspect of a believer's life. Rooted in biblical teachings and exemplified by figures like Abraham and Moses, faith is essential for salvation and daily living, providing strength, guidance, and assurance in God's unchanging nature and promises.

Hope: A Multifaceted Concept

Hope in Christianity is a profound and multifaceted concept that plays a crucial role in the lives of believers. It is rooted in the expectation of a better future in this life and the afterlife. It serves as a source of strength, optimism, and resilience. Here's a deeper exploration of the concept of hope in Christianity:

Theological Foundation of Hope: Hope in Christianity is grounded in the promises of God, as revealed in the Bible. It is the confident expectation that God's promises will be fulfilled. This includes the assurance of salvation, the promise of eternal life, and the belief that God is sovereign and has a perfect plan for each person.

Biblical References: Several biblical passages underscore the importance of hope. For instance, Romans 15:13 states, "May the God of hope fill you with all joy and peace as you trust in him, so that you may overflow with hope by the power of the Holy Spirit." This verse highlights that hope is not just an abstract concept but is deeply tied to joy, peace, and the work of the Holy Spirit.

Hope in Times of Suffering: Christian hope is particularly significant in times of suffering and adversity. It offers believers a perspective that transcends present difficulties, rooted in the belief that God works through all circumstances for the greater good. Romans 8:28 reinforces this: "And we know that in all things God works for the good of those who love him, who have been called according to his purpose."

Hope and the Resurrection: The resurrection of Jesus Christ is central to Christian hope. It is the ultimate demonstration of God's power over death and the promise of new life. 1 Peter 1:3 states, "Praise be to the God and Father of our Lord Jesus Christ! In his great mercy, he has given us new birth into a living hope through the resurrection of Jesus Christ from the dead."

Hope and Eternal Life: Hope in Christianity extends beyond this life to the promise of eternal life with God. This eternal perspective gives believers the strength to endure life's challenges, knowing their ultimate destiny is secure. John 3:16 encapsulates this promise: "For God so loved the world that he gave his one and only Son, that whoever believes in him shall not perish but have eternal life."

Practical Implications of Hope: Christian hope is not passive but actively shapes believers' lives. It inspires acts of love, service, and perseverance. Hope motivates Christians to make positive changes in their lives and the world, reflecting God's love and justice.

Encouragement and Community: Hope is also a communal experience. Christians are encouraged to support and uplift one another, sharing their hope in Christ. Hebrews 10:23-24 urges believers to "hold unswervingly to the hope we profess, for he who promised is faithful. And let us consider how we may spur one another toward love and good deeds."

Hope and Resilience: Hope fosters resilience by providing a firm foundation in times of uncertainty and trial. It reassures believers that their struggles are temporary and that God's purposes will ultimately prevail. This resilience is evident in many Christians who, despite facing immense challenges, maintain their faith and trust God's plan.

Hope as a Witness: The hopeful outlook of Christians can serve as a powerful witness to others. In a world often marked by despair and hopelessness, Christians' hope can draw others to the faith, demonstrating the transformative power of a relationship with God.

Personal Reflection: Believers are encouraged to reflect on and renew their hope continually. This involves engaging with Scripture, prayer, and worship, allowing God to strengthen and sustain their hope. Personal testimonies and stories of faith can also serve as reminders of God's faithfulness and the hope available to all.

By embodying hope, Christians can navigate life's challenges with purpose and assurance, trusting in God's promises and looking forward to a future filled with His love and presence.

Charity: Love In Action

Charity, often called "love in action," is fundamental to Christian life and teachings. It embodies the principle of giving selflessly to those in need, reflecting the unconditional love that God shows to humanity. Here's an in-depth look at the concept of charity in Christianity:

Biblical Foundation of Charity

Charity is deeply rooted in biblical teachings. The New Testament emphasizes loving one's neighbor and helping those in need. Jesus' teachings, particularly in the parable of the Good Samaritan (Luke 10:25-37), highlight the call to love and care for others, regardless of their background or circumstances.

Charity as a Reflection of God's Love

Charity is seen as a reflection of God's love for humanity. Christians believe that by showing charity, they are embodying God's love and compassion. This is exemplified in 1 John 4:19, which states, "We love because he first loved us."

Forms of Charity

Charity can manifest in various forms, including:

Financial Assistance: Donating money to individuals, charities, or organizations that support those in need.

Time and Service: Volunteering time and skills to help others, such as serving in soup kitchens, mentoring, or participating in community service projects.

Emotional Support: Offering a listening ear, companionship, and emotional support to those who are lonely, grieving, or struggling with personal issues.

Material Donations: Providing food, clothing, shelter, and other essential items to those who lack basic necessities.

The Spirit of Giving

True charity involves giving without expecting anything in return. It is an act of selflessness motivated by genuine concern and compassion for others. 2 Corinthians 9:7 highlights this spirit, stating, "Each of you should give what you have decided in your heart to give, not reluctantly or under compulsion, for God loves a cheerful giver."

Charity and Social Justice

Charity in Christianity is about alleviating immediate needs and addressing systemic issues that cause poverty and injustice. This involves advocating for social justice, supporting fair policies, and working towards creating a more equitable society.

Personal Transformation Through Charity

Engaging in charitable acts can lead to personal growth and transformation. It fosters humility, empathy, and a sense of community. By focusing on the needs of others, individuals can develop a deeper understanding of their blessings and cultivate a spirit of gratitude and generosity.

Impact on Recipients

Charity has a profound impact on those who receive it. It can provide relief, hope, and a sense of dignity to individuals facing hardships. Knowing someone cares and is willing to help can make a significant difference in their lives.

Encouraging a Culture of Charity

Christian communities often encourage a culture of charity through organized events, fundraisers, and volunteer opportunities. Churches and faith-based organizations are crucial in mobilizing resources and volunteers to support various charitable initiatives.

Challenges of Charity

While charity is essential, it also comes with challenges. It's crucial to ensure that charitable efforts are respectful and empowering rather than creating dependency or undermining the dignity of those being helped. Sustainable and thoughtful approaches to charity can make a lasting impact.

Charity as a Witness to Faith

Acts of charity serve as a powerful witness to the Christian faith. They demonstrate the love and compassion at the heart of Christianity, attracting others to the faith through selfless giving and kindness.

Key Scriptural References

Matthew 25:35-40: "For I was hungry, and you gave me something to eat, I was thirsty, and you gave me something to drink, I was a stranger, and you invited me in, I needed clothes, and you clothed me, I was sick, and you looked after me, I was in prison, and you came to visit me."

James 2:15-17: "Suppose a brother or a sister is without clothes and daily food. If one of you says to them, 'Go in peace; keep warm and well fed,' but does nothing about their physical needs, what good is it? In the same way, if it is not accompanied by action, faith by itself is dead."

By embracing and practicing charity, Christians can live out the teachings of Jesus, making a tangible difference in the lives of others and contributing to a more compassionate and just world.

Community: The Cornerstone Of Christian Life

Community is a cornerstone of Christian life, playing a crucial role in fostering fellowship, support, and accountability among believers. Here's an in-depth look at the significance of community in Christianity:

Biblical Foundation of Community: The Bible emphasizes the importance of community and collective worship. Acts 2:42-47 describes the early Christian community as one where believers devoted themselves to the apostles' teaching, fellowship, breaking bread, and prayer. This passage highlights the communal nature of Christian worship and living.

The Church as a Family: In Christianity, the church is often called the family of God. This familial imagery underscores members' sense of belonging, care, and mutual responsibility. Just as a family supports and nurtures its members, the church community provides spiritual, emotional, and sometimes material support.

Fellowship: Fellowship, or "koinonia" in Greek, is a crucial aspect of the Christian community. It involves sharing life together, encouraging one another, and growing in faith collectively. Regular gatherings for worship, Bible study, prayer meetings, and social activities help build strong relationships and a sense of unity among believers.

Support System: The Christian community serves as a support system, offering help in times of need. This can include providing meals for the sick, visiting those in prison, offering financial assistance to those in hardship, and providing emotional support during difficult times. Galatians 6:2 exhorts believers to "Carry each other's burdens, and in this way, you will fulfill the law of Christ."

Accountability: Being part of a Christian community involves mutual accountability. Fellow believers help each other stay true to their faith, providing correction, encouragement, and guidance. James 5:16 encourages this practice: "Therefore confess your sins to each other and pray for each other so that you may be healed."

Spiritual Growth: Community is vital for spiritual growth. It provides a context for learning, discipleship, and developing spiritual gifts. Through sermons, Bible studies, and discussions, believers can deepen their understanding of Scripture and grow in their relationship with God.

Collective Worship: Worshiping strengthens the faith of individual believers and the community. Singing, praying, and partaking in sacraments like Communion are potent expressions of collective faith that reinforce a sense of shared belief and purpose.

Encouragement and Edification: The Christian community is a source of encouragement and edification. Hebrews 10:24-25 urges believers to "spur one another on toward love and good deeds, not giving up meeting together, as some are in the habit of doing, but encouraging one another." This encouragement helps believers persevere in their faith.

Service and Outreach: Communities of faith often engage in service and outreach, extending their support beyond the church walls to the broader community. This can include mission work, charitable activities, and social justice initiatives. Such efforts reflect the love of Christ and serve as a witness to non-believers.

Unity in Diversity: Christian communities are diverse, encompassing people from various backgrounds, cultures, and walks of life. This diversity reflects the church's universal nature and the gospel's inclusive message—Ephesians 4:3-6 calls for maintaining unity in the Spirit, acknowledging one body and one Spirit.

Examples of Community in Action

Small Groups: Many churches have small groups or home fellowships where members meet regularly to study the Bible, pray, and support one another.

Service Teams: Volunteer groups within the church that engage in various service forms, from helping with church events to community outreach.

Support Groups: Specialized groups that support specific needs, such as grief counseling, addiction recovery, or marriage enrichment.

Challenges and Opportunities

Challenges: Building and maintaining a healthy community can be challenging due to differences in opinions, personality conflicts, and logistical issues. Effective communication, empathy, and a focus on shared faith can help overcome these challenges.

Opportunities: Strong communities can serve as powerful witnesses to the love and unity found in Christ. They provide a safe space for growth, healing, and transformation, making the church a beacon of hope in the broader society.

Key Scriptural References

Romans 12:4-5: "For just as each of us has one body with many members, and these members do not all have the same function, so in Christ we, though many, form one body, and each member belongs to all the others."

1 Corinthians 12:25-27: "So that there should be no division in the body, but that its parts should have equal concern for each other. If one part suffers, every part suffers; if one part is honored, every part rejoices. Now you are the body of Christ, and each one of you is a part of it."

In summary, community is integral to Christian life, providing a support system, fostering spiritual growth, and enabling collective worship and service. It embodies the biblical principles of love, unity, and mutual support, helping believers live out their faith in tangible and impactful ways.

Integrity: Aligning One's Actions With One's Beliefs

Integrity in Christianity is about aligning one's actions with one's beliefs and living out the teachings of Christ with honesty and steadfastness. It's about being authentic, consistent, and accurate to one's faith in every aspect of life. Here's a deeper exploration of the concept of integrity within the Christian context:

Biblical Foundation of Integrity: The Bible emphasizes integrity as a vital characteristic for believers. Proverbs 10:9 states, "Whoever walks in integrity walks securely, but whoever takes crooked paths will be found out." This highlights the security and stability of living a life of integrity.

Consistency with Christian Teachings: Integrity means a Christian's actions reflect their beliefs. This involves adhering to the moral and ethical teachings of the Bible in all areas of life, not just when it's convenient or when others are watching. James 1:22 encourages believers to "Do not merely listen to the word, and deceive yourselves. Do what it says."

Honesty and Transparency: Living with integrity involves being honest and transparent in all dealings. This includes speaking truthfully, avoiding deceit, and being forthcoming in one's interactions. Ephesians 4:25 urges, "Therefore each of you must put off falsehood and speak truthfully to your neighbor, for we are all members of one body."

Standing by One's Principles: Integrity requires standing by one's principles, even in adversity or temptation. This means making ethical decisions based on Christian values, even when difficult or unpopular. Daniel's unwavering faith and refusal to bow to the king's decree, as described in the Book of Daniel, is a profound example of this steadfastness.

Doing the Right Thing When No One is Watching: An essential aspect of integrity is doing what is right even when no one else sees it. This aligns with the understanding that God sees all actions and intentions. Colossians 3:23-24 advises, "Whatever you do, work at it with all your heart, as working for the Lord, not for human masters, since you know that you will receive an inheritance from the Lord as a reward."

Personal and Spiritual Growth: Living with integrity fosters personal and spiritual growth. It helps believers develop a solid moral compass and build character. This growth is reflected in how they handle challenges, interact with others, and maintain their commitment to their faith.

Integrity in Relationships: Integrity affects all relationships, whether personal, professional, or communal. It builds trust and respect, as others can rely on a person of integrity to be honest, fair, and consistent. This trust is foundational for healthy and meaningful relationships.

Witness to Others: A life of integrity is a powerful witness to others. Christians living out their faith honestly and consistently demonstrate the gospel's transformative power. Matthew 5:16 encourages believers to "let your light shine before others that they may see your good deeds and glorify your Father in heaven."

Accountability: Integrity also involves accountability. Christians are called to hold each other accountable to live lives that honor God. This accountability can take the form of mentorship, confession, and mutual support within the Christian community.

Challenges to Integrity: Maintaining integrity can be challenging, especially in a world that values success over ethics. Christians may face temptations to compromise their principles for personal gain, peer pressure, or societal acceptance. Staying true to one's faith requires courage, resilience, and reliance on God's strength.

Rewards of Integrity: The rewards of living a life of integrity are manifold. These include a clear conscience, peace of mind, respect from others, and ultimately, God's approval. Proverbs 11:3 says, "The integrity of the upright guides them, but the unfaithful are destroyed by their duplicity."

Practical Steps to Cultivate Integrity:

Regular Self-Reflection: Examine your actions and motives to ensure they align with your Christian values.

Prayer and Study: Engage in prayer and study of the Scriptures to strengthen your understanding and commitment to living a life of integrity.

Seek Accountability: Build relationships with other believers who can support and hold you accountable.

Confession and Repentance: Be willing to admit when you fall short and seek forgiveness and guidance from God and others.

Key Scriptural References:

Psalm 25:21: "May integrity and uprightness protect me, because my hope, Lord, is in you."

Titus 2:7-8: "In everything set them an example by doing what is good. In your teaching, show integrity, seriousness, and soundness of speech that cannot be condemned so that those who oppose you may be ashamed because they have nothing bad to say about us."

In summary, integrity in Christianity is about living a life that faithfully reflects the teachings of Christ. It involves honesty, consistency, and a commitment to doing what is right, even facing challenges. By cultivating integrity, believers can grow spiritually, build trust in their relationships, and serve as powerful witnesses to the truth and love of God.

Peace: A Fundamental Value

Peace is a fundamental Christian value, deeply rooted in the teachings of Jesus Christ, who is often called the "Prince of Peace." The concept of peace in Christianity goes beyond the mere absence of conflict; it encompasses inner tranquility, harmonious relationships, and a commitment to justice and reconciliation. Here's a detailed exploration of peace as a Christian value:

Biblical Foundation of Peace: The Bible is replete with references to peace. In the Old Testament, peace (shalom in Hebrew) signifies completeness, welfare, and harmony. In the New Testament, Jesus' teachings and actions emphasize peace as a core element of the Christian life. Isaiah 9:6 prophesies Jesus as the "Prince of Peace," highlighting the centrality of peace in his mission.

Jesus as the Prince of Peace: Jesus' life and teachings exemplify peace. He taught love for enemies (Matthew 5:44), blessed peacemakers (Matthew 5:9), and promoted reconciliation (Matthew 5:23-24). His calming of the storm (Mark 4:39) and his words to his disciples, "Peace I leave with you; my peace I give you" (John 14:27), underscore his role as the bringer of peace.

Inner Peace: Christianity emphasizes inner peace, which comes from a relationship with God. Philippians 4:6-7 advises believers to present their requests to God with thanksgiving, promising that "the peace of God, which transcends all understanding, will guard your hearts and your minds in Christ Jesus." This inner peace depends not on external circumstances but trust in God's sovereignty and love.

Peace in Relationships: Christians are called to live in peace with others. Romans 12:18 instructs, "If it is possible, as far as it depends on you, live at peace with everyone." This involves practicing forgiveness, seeking reconciliation, and resolving conflicts amicably. Colossians 3:13 emphasizes bearing with each other and forgiving grievances.

Peacemaking: Peacemaking is an active pursuit of harmony and justice. Matthew 5:9 blesses the peacemakers, "for they will be called children of God." Peacemaking involves addressing the root causes of conflict, advocating for justice, and promoting understanding and cooperation. This can extend to various areas of life, including family, community, and international relations.

Reconciliation: Reconciliation is central to Christian peace. It involves restoring broken relationships with God and others. 2 Corinthians 5:18-19 speaks of the ministry of reconciliation given to believers, urging them to be agents of reconciliation in the world, reflecting God's reconciling work through Christ.

Peace and Justice: True peace in Christianity is inseparable from justice. The Bible calls for fair treatment of all people and standing up against oppression and inequality. Isaiah 32:17 states, "The fruit of that righteousness will be peace; its effect will be quietness and confidence forever." This underscores that lasting peace is built on the foundation of justice.

Community and Global Peace: Christianity encourages efforts toward peace within communities and globally. The teachings of Christ inspire initiatives for social justice, conflict resolution, and humanitarian aid. Christians are called to be instruments of peace in a world often marked by division and strife.

Peace in Worship: Worship in the Christian context often includes prayers and hymns that reflect the desire for peace. Though not directly from the Bible, the "Peace Prayer of Saint Francis" beautifully encapsulates this aspiration: "Lord, make me an instrument of your peace. Where there is hatred, let me sow love."

Peace and Spiritual Warfare: Christianity also acknowledges spiritual warfare while promoting peace. Ephesians 6:12 speaks of the struggle against the spiritual forces of evil. However, even in this context, believers are encouraged to stand firm in faith and rely on God's power, seeking peace amid spiritual battles.

Practical Steps to Cultivate Peace:

Prayer and Meditation: Regular prayer and meditation on Scripture can help cultivate inner peace and a peaceful mindset.

Conflict Resolution: Actively resolve conflicts through dialogue, forgiveness, and understanding.

Acts of Kindness: Engage in acts of kindness and service that promote harmony and goodwill.

Advocacy: Advocate for social justice and resolve systemic issues hindering peace.

Community Involvement: Participate in community activities that foster unity and cooperation.

Key Scriptural References:

Matthew 5:9: "Blessed are the peacemakers, for they will be called children of God."

Romans 12:18: "If it is possible, as far as it depends on you, live at peace with everyone."

Philippians 4:6-7: "Do not be anxious about anything, but in every situation, by prayer and petition, with thanksgiving, present your requests to God. And the peace of God, which transcends all understanding, will guard your hearts and minds in Christ Jesus."

Examples of Peace in Action:

Personal Life: Cultivating inner peace through prayer and mindfulness, resolving conflicts amicably, and practicing forgiveness.

Community Engagement: Participating in peacebuilding activities, supporting social justice initiatives, and helping to mediate disputes.

Global Efforts: Supporting international peace efforts, such as missions, humanitarian aid, and advocacy for oppressed groups.

In summary, peace in Christianity is a comprehensive value that involves inner tranquility, harmonious relationships, active peacemaking, and a commitment to justice. It reflects the life and teachings of Jesus Christ. It calls believers to be agents of peace in their personal lives, communities, and the world.

.

These values guide Christians daily, shaping their interactions with others and their relationship with God. They foster a world marked by love, acceptance, and mutual respect when genuinely understood and practiced.

Doing The Devil's Work Behind The Christian Mask

"Doing the devil's work behind the Christian mask" refers to the deceptive practice of professing Christian beliefs or appearing pious while engaging in actions or behaviors contrary to Christian values. It involves hypocrisy and deceit, where individuals conceal their true intentions or engage in wrongdoing while presenting a facade of righteousness. This concept resonates with Jesus's teachings, particularly his condemnation of religious hypocrisy and outward displays of piety that mask inner corruption.

Biblical Context

Jesus frequently addressed the issue of hypocrisy among religious leaders during his ministry:

Matthew 23: In this chapter, known as the "Seven Woes," Jesus denounces the scribes and Pharisees for their hypocrisy, calling them "whitewashed tombs" that appear beautiful on the outside but are full of dead men's bones and uncleanness on the inside.

Luke 11:39-44: Jesus rebukes the Pharisees for their emphasis on outward rituals while neglecting justice and the love of God.

Exploitation

Examples of "Devil's Work" Behind the Mask

Exploitation: Some individuals may exploit their position within Christian communities for personal gain, financial or otherwise while maintaining a veneer of piety.

Manipulation: Using religious language or symbols to manipulate others for selfish purposes, such as exerting control or gaining influence.

Judgment and Condemnation: Judgment and Condemnation: Condemning others under religious righteousness while harboring bitterness, prejudice, or hatred in their hearts.

Abuse: Abuse: Engaging in abusive behavior, whether emotional, physical, or spiritual, while claiming to represent Christian values of love and compassion.

Hypocrisy: Hypocrisy: Living a double life, professing Christian beliefs publicly but behaving differently in private, with actions that contradict those beliefs.

Consequences And Impact

Undermining Trust: Such actions erode trust within Christian communities and tarnish the reputation of Christianity as a whole.

Spiritual Harm: Individuals affected by hypocrisy may experience spiritual confusion, disillusionment, or trauma, leading to a loss of faith or a distorted view of Christianity.

Social and Moral Decay: Hypocrisy within religious institutions can contribute to broader societal cynicism and moral decline as people become disillusioned with institutions they once trusted.

Guarding Against Hypocrisy

Authenticity: Cultivating genuine faith and sincerity in one's beliefs, aligning actions with professed values.

Accountability: Surrounding oneself with honest and trustworthy individuals who hold one another accountable for their actions.

Humility: Recognizing one's fallibility and vulnerability to temptation, seeking forgiveness and grace when needed.

Transparency: Being open and honest about struggles and failures rather than hiding behind a facade of perfection.

Restoring Integrity

Repentance: Acknowledging wrongdoing, seeking forgiveness from God and those harmed, and committing to genuine change.

Amends: Taking concrete steps to repair the harm caused, such as restitution, reconciliation, and addressing systemic issues.

Renewal: Embracing a renewed commitment to authentic faith and ethical conduct grounded in humility, compassion, and love.

In summary, "doing the devil's work behind the Christian mask" reflects the insidious nature of hypocrisy within religious contexts. It highlights the importance of sincerity, integrity, and accountability in living out Christian values and the damaging effects of hypocrisy on individuals and communities. By confronting hypocrisy with honesty, humility, and a commitment to genuine faith, individuals and communities can strive for greater authenticity and integrity in their Christian witness.

Consequences And Impact

Undermining Trust: Undermining Trust: Such actions erode trust within Christian communities and tarnish the reputation of Christianity as a whole.

Spiritual Harm: Spiritual Harm: Individuals affected by hypocrisy may experience spiritual confusion, disillusionment, or trauma, leading to a loss of faith or a distorted view of Christianity.

Social and Moral Decay: Hypocrisy within religious institutions can contribute to broader societal cynicism and moral decline as people become disillusioned with institutions they once trusted.

Guarding Against Hypocrisy: Guarding Against Hypocrisy

Authenticity: Cultivating genuine faith and sincerity in one's beliefs, aligning actions with professed values.

Accountability: Accountability: Surrounding oneself with honest and trustworthy individuals who hold one another accountable for their actions.

Humility: Recognizing one's fallibility and vulnerability to temptation, seeking forgiveness and grace when needed.

Transparency: Transparency: Being open and honest about struggles and failures rather than hiding behind a facade of perfection.

Restoring Integrity

Repentance: Acknowledging wrongdoing, seeking forgiveness from God and those harmed, and committing to genuine change.

DOING THE DEVIL'S WORK BEHIND THE CHRISTIAN MASK

Amends: Amends: Taking concrete steps to repair the harm caused, such as restitution, reconciliation, and addressing systemic issues.

Renewal: Embracing a renewed commitment to authentic faith and ethical conduct grounded in humility, compassion, and love.

In summary, "doing the devil's work behind the Christian mask" reflects the insidious nature of hypocrisy within religious contexts. It highlights the importance of sincerity, integrity, and accountability in living out Christian values and the damaging effects of hypocrisy on individuals and communities. By confronting hypocrisy with honesty, humility, and a commitment to genuine faith, individuals and communities can strive for greater authenticity and integrity in their Christian witness.

Contradictions In Christian Behavior

Setting The Stage: Contradictions In Christian Behavior

"Setting the stage: Contradictions in Christian behavior" refers to the discrepancy between professed Christian beliefs and the actions or behaviors of some individuals who identify as Christians. This concept acknowledges the presence of inconsistencies or contradictions in how some Christians live out their faith, which can lead to confusion, skepticism, or criticism both within and outside of Christian communities.

Recognition Of Contradictions

Professed Values vs. Actions: Some Christians may proclaim love, compassion, and forgiveness but fail to demonstrate these qualities consistently in their interactions with others.

Scriptural Teachings vs. Interpretation: There may be discrepancies between the teachings of Jesus and other biblical figures and how individuals interpret and apply these teachings in their lives.

Church Doctrine vs. Personal Beliefs: Disagreements or inconsistencies between official church doctrine and individual Christians' personal beliefs or practices may arise.

Community Ideals vs. Reality: Christian communities may espouse ideals of unity, acceptance, and support, but interpersonal conflicts, divisions, or exclusions may occur in practice.

Perceived Hypocrisy: Instances of hypocrisy, where individuals act in ways that contradict their professed beliefs, can undermine the credibility of Christian witness.

Potential Factors Contributing To Contradictions

Human Fallibility: Christians, like all individuals, are fallible and prone to imperfection, leading to inconsistencies between belief and behavior.

Cultural Influences: Societal norms, pressures, and cultural values may sometimes conflict with Christian principles, leading to tension or compromise.

Misinterpretation or Misapplication: Misunderstandings or misapplications of biblical teachings may lead to behaviors that diverge from the intended message of Christianity.

Spiritual Struggles: Christians may grapple with personal challenges, doubts, or temptations that affect their behavior and choices.

Institutional Dynamics: Organizational structures, power dynamics, and institutional priorities within churches or Christian institutions may contribute to contradictions or ethical lapses.

Navigating Contradictions

Critical Reflection: Christians are encouraged to critically examine their beliefs and behaviors in light of biblical teachings, seeking to align their actions with their professed values.

Community Accountability: Mutual accountability within Christian communities can help identify and address contradictions, fostering growth and accountability.

Humility and Repentance: Acknowledging shortcomings and seeking forgiveness and reconciliation are essential to Christian faith and practice.

Seeking Guidance: Consulting trusted spiritual mentors, pastors, or theologians can provide guidance and support in navigating complex ethical or theological questions.

Continuous Growth: Recognizing that the Christian faith is a journey of growth and transformation, individuals are encouraged to strive for greater consistency and integrity in their beliefs and actions.

Addressing Skepticism And Criticism

Transparency: Openness and transparency about struggles, doubts, and failures can foster understanding and empathy, mitigating perceptions of hypocrisy.

Demonstrating Authenticity: Authenticity and humility in acknowledging imperfections and striving for growth can enhance the credibility of Christian witness.

Reconciliation and Restoration: Addressing harm or damage caused by contradictions through sincere efforts toward reconciliation and restoration can help rebuild trust and credibility.

Promoting Positive Change: Individuals and communities committed to addressing contradictions can work toward positive change within themselves and society.

Recognizing and addressing contradictions in Christian behavior is essential for fostering authenticity, integrity, and credibility within Christian communities. By confronting inconsistencies with humility, reflection, and accountability, Christians can strive for greater alignment between their beliefs and actions, ultimately reflecting the transformative power of the Christian faith in their lives and interactions with others.

Questioning The Disconnect Between Professed Beliefs And Actions

"Questioning the disconnect between professed beliefs and actions" involves examining discrepancies or inconsistencies when individuals or groups profess certain beliefs or values. Yet, their actions fail to align with these professed ideals. This concept explores the tension between what is claimed or preached and what is practiced, prompting critical reflection on the authenticity and integrity of belief systems and behaviors.

Identification Of Disconnect

Professed Values vs. Actions: Individuals or groups may proclaim specific values or principles, such as love, honesty, or compassion, but their actions may not consistently reflect these professed beliefs.

Religious Teachings vs. Behavior: Discrepancies may arise between the teachings of a particular religion or belief system and the conduct of its adherents.

Ethical Dilemmas: Situations may arise where individuals face moral or ethical dilemmas, leading to actions that diverge from their stated beliefs or values.

Public Image vs. Private Reality: There may be disparities between individuals' or groups' public persona or image and the reality of their private behavior or attitudes.

Hypocrisy: Instances of hypocrisy, where individuals or groups advocate one set of standards while engaging in behavior that contradicts those standards, may be observed.

Examination Of Causes

Individual Factors: Personal motives, desires, fears, or weaknesses may influence behavior, leading individuals to act in ways that contradict their beliefs.

Social and Cultural Influences: Societal norms, peer pressure, or cultural expectations may pressure individuals to conform to certain behaviors, even if they conflict with their personal beliefs.

Psychological Factors: Cognitive biases, rationalizations, or self-deception may contribute to individuals justifying their actions in ways that minimize or ignore the disconnect between beliefs and actions.

Institutional Dynamics: Organizational structures, power dynamics, or institutional priorities within religious, political, or social institutions may create environments where the disconnect between professed beliefs and actions is more pronounced.

Complexity of Human Nature: Human beings are complex, multifaceted beings capable of holding contradictory beliefs or engaging in behavior that may seem inconsistent or paradoxical.

Challenges And Consequences

Cognitive Dissonance: Individuals may experience discomfort or cognitive dissonance when confronted with the mismatch between their professed beliefs and actions.

Loss of Trust: Disconnects between beliefs and actions can erode trust within individual relationships and broader social or institutional contexts.

Impact on Credibility: Individuals or groups may suffer reputational damage or loss of credibility if perceived as hypocritical or insincere in their professed beliefs.

Missed Opportunities for Growth: Failure to address discrepancies between beliefs and actions may hinder personal or collective growth, as opportunities for self-reflection and improvement are overlooked.

The undermining of Values: Persistent disconnects between professed beliefs and actions can lead to cynicism, disillusionment, or apathy, undermining the perceived validity or relevance of the values or principles being espoused.

Navigating The Disconnect

Critical Reflection: Individuals and groups are encouraged to reflect critically, examining the reasons behind the disconnect between professed beliefs and actions.

Alignment and Integration: Efforts should be made to align beliefs, values, and actions, fostering greater integrity and consistency in behavior.

Accountability: Holding oneself and others accountable for their actions and commitments can help address discrepancies and promote ethical behavior.

Open Dialogue: Creating spaces for open dialogue and honest communication allows individuals to explore and address discrepancies in beliefs and actions without fear of judgment.

Commitment to Growth: Embracing a growth mindset and a willingness to learn from mistakes can facilitate personal and collective growth, leading to greater alignment between beliefs and actions.

In summary, questioning the disconnect between professed beliefs and actions involves critically examining inconsistencies or contradictions that may arise in individual or collective behavior. By acknowledging and addressing these discrepancies with honesty, humility, and a commitment to growth, individuals and groups can strive for greater integrity, authenticity, and alignment between what they profess to believe and how they behave in practice.

Introduction To The Central Thesis: Christianity As A

Mask For Personal Failings

The central thesis of "Christianity as a mask for personal failings" posits that some individuals may use Christianity or its outward expressions as a facade to conceal or justify their personal failings, shortcomings, or unethical behaviors. This concept suggests that rather than embodying the values and teachings of Christianity authentically. These individuals may adopt a superficial adherence to religious practices or beliefs to mask their flaws or evade accountability for their actions.

Introduction To The Thesis

The backdrop of Christian Ethics: Christianity espouses principles of love, forgiveness, humility, and moral integrity, as exemplified in the teachings of Jesus Christ and the ethical precepts of the Bible.

Observation of Hypocrisy: Despite these lofty ideals, instances of hypocrisy, moral failure, or ethical misconduct among individuals who profess to be Christians are not uncommon.

Exploring Motivations: This thesis examines the underlying motivations and dynamics that may lead some individuals to use Christianity as a shield or pretext for their failures.

Challenges to Authenticity: The thesis questions the authenticity of professed religious beliefs and practices when they deflect attention from or justify individuals' moral shortcomings.

Implications for Understanding: Understanding how Christianity can be co-opted as a mask for personal failings sheds light on broader issues of integrity, accountability, and the genuine pursuit of spiritual values.

Key Themes

Hypocrisy and Deception: Individuals may engage in deceptive practices or adopt a hypocritical stance, presenting themselves as devout Christians while engaging in behavior that contradicts Christian principles.

Evasion of Responsibility: Rather than confronting and addressing their failings, individuals may use Christianity as a scapegoat or pretext to evade responsibility or accountability for their actions.

Moral Relativism: The thesis explores the phenomenon of moral relativism, where individuals may selectively interpret or cherry-pick religious teachings to justify their behaviors or rationalize their ethical lapses.

Psychological Dynamics: Psychological factors such as cognitive dissonance, self-deception, or a desire for social approval may contribute to individuals' propensity to use Christianity as a mask for personal failings.

Impact on Faith Communities: The thesis considers the broader implications for faith communities, including the erosion of trust, disillusionment among believers, and the tarnishing of Christianity's reputation when perceived as a vehicle for hypocrisy or moral bankruptcy.

Navigating The Thesis

Critical Analysis: Engaging in critical analysis and introspection enables individuals to examine the authenticity of their religious beliefs and practices, discerning whether they genuinely reflect their values or serve as a veneer for personal failings.

Promoting Integrity: Emphasizing integrity, humility, and self-awareness within religious communities fosters an environment where individuals feel empowered to acknowledge and address their imperfections honestly.

Accountability and Support: Establishing mechanisms for accountability and support within faith communities encourages individuals to confront their failings with courage and seek assistance in their journey toward personal growth and moral development.

Reclaiming Authenticity: By reclaiming authenticity and sincerity in their religious beliefs and practices, individuals can cultivate a genuine expression of Christianity grounded in humility, compassion, and ethical integrity.

Ethical Reflection: Engaging in ongoing ethical reflection and dialogue fosters a deeper understanding of the ethical dimensions of Christianity and promotes a more robust commitment to living out its values authentically in everyday life.

In summary, "Christianity as a mask for personal failings" challenges individuals to critically examine the authenticity of their religious beliefs and practices, encouraging them to confront their moral shortcomings with honesty and humility. By interrogating the motives behind superficial adherence to Christianity and promoting genuine integrity and ethical accountability, individuals can strive for a more authentic expression of their faith that reflects the transformative power of Christian values in their lives.

Ask Yourself If You Are A True Christian, Or Are You Doing The Devil's Work Behind The Christian Mask?

Reflecting on whether one is living according to Christian principles or engaging in behaviors contradicting those principles is essential to spiritual growth and integrity. It involves introspection, self-awareness, and a willingness to confront one's actions and motivations honestly.

Asking oneself if they are a faithful Christian or if one is doing the Devil's work behind the Christian mask requires a deep examination of one's beliefs, attitudes, and actions. It prompts individuals to assess whether their behaviors align with the teachings of Jesus Christ, such as love, compassion, humility, forgiveness, and justice, or if they are driven by selfishness, pride, greed, or malice.

To determine whether one is truly living as a Christian or if they are masking harmful intentions with religious pretenses, individuals may consider the following questions:

- Am I acting out of genuine love and compassion for others, or am I motivated by self-interest and pride?
- Do my actions reflect humility and servant-heartedness, or do they seek to elevate myself at the expense of others?
- Am I willing to forgive those who wrong me and extend grace and mercy, or do I hold onto grudges and seek vengeance?
- Do I seek justice and fairness for all people, especially the marginalized and oppressed, or do I perpetuate injustice and discrimination?
- Are my words and actions consistent with the values and teachings of Jesus Christ, or do they contradict his message of love, acceptance, and righteousness?
- Am I using my religious beliefs and practices as a mask to hide immoral behavior or justify harmful actions, or do I genuinely strive

to live with integrity and authenticity?

- Do I engage in self-reflection and seek to grow spiritually, or do I remain stagnant in my faith and resistant to change?
- Am I treating others with respect and dignity, recognizing their inherent worth as fellow human beings created in the image of God, or do I demean or belittle them for my satisfaction or gain?
- Do I actively seek to understand and empathize with the experiences and perspectives of others, especially those who are different from me, or do I remain closed off and judgmental?
- Am I quick to extend a helping hand to those in need, offering support, encouragement, and practical assistance, or do I turn a blind eye to their suffering and prioritize my comfort and convenience?
- Do I practice honesty and integrity in all my dealings, striving to be truthful and trustworthy in my words and actions, or do I engage in deceit, manipulation, or dishonesty for personal gain?
- Am I open to feedback and correction from others, recognizing my fallibility and the need for accountability, or do I resist criticism and refuse to acknowledge my mistakes or shortcomings?
- Do I prioritize spiritual growth and the pursuit of holiness, seeking to cultivate virtues such as patience, kindness, and self-control, or do I neglect my spiritual life and indulge in sinful or destructive behaviors?
- Am I actively engaged in building and nurturing authentic relationships with God and others, fostering connections based on love, trust, and mutual respect, or do I prioritize superficial or self-serving interactions?
- Do I use my influence and resources to advocate for justice, equality, and the common good, working to address systemic injustices and alleviate suffering, or do I remain complacent and indifferent to the needs and struggles of others?
- Am I willing to challenge societal norms and cultural practices that conflict with Christian values, speaking out against oppression, discrimination, and injustice, or do I passively conform to the status quo and perpetuate harmful ideologies?
- Do I recognize the importance of self-care and self-reflection in

maintaining emotional, mental, and spiritual well-being, prioritizing rest, renewal, and self-awareness, or do I neglect my needs and allow stress, anxiety, and burnout to dominate my life?

- Am I committed to living a life of authenticity and transparency, embracing vulnerability and imperfection, or do I hide behind a façade of piety and perfectionism, afraid to acknowledge my struggles and weaknesses?

- Am I actively fostering unity and reconciliation within the Christian community, seeking to build bridges and mend divisions, or am I contributing to conflict, division, and discord?

- Do I prioritize cultivating a spirit of gratitude and contentment, recognizing and appreciating God's blessings, or do I succumb to envy greed, and a constant craving for more?

- Am I committed to stewardship and care for God's creation, recognizing the importance of environmental sustainability and responsibility, or do I neglect my role as a caretaker of the Earth?

- Do I demonstrate a willingness to learn and grow in understanding God's Word and His will for my life, remaining open to new insights and perspectives, or do I cling rigidly to my interpretations and traditions?

- Am I actively serving and ministering to others, using my gifts and talents to meet the needs of those around me, or do I prioritize my desires and ambitions above others?

- Do I practice discernment and critical thinking in evaluating spiritual teachings and practices, being cautious of false doctrines and misleading interpretations, or do popular trends and charismatic personalities easily sway me?

- Am I cultivating a spirit of generosity and sacrificial giving, freely sharing my resources and blessings with others, or do I hoard my wealth and possessions out of fear or selfishness?

- Do I prioritize prayer and communion with God, seeking His guidance and wisdom in all aspects of my life, or do I rely solely on my understanding and strength?

- Am I actively engaged in advocating for the marginalized and vulnerable in society, standing up for the rights and dignity of all people, or do I remain silent in the face of injustice and oppression?

- Do I practice self-examination and repentance, acknowledge and confess my sins before God and others, or justify or excuse my wrongdoing?
- Am I committed to fostering a culture of grace and forgiveness, extending mercy and compassion to those who have wronged me, or do I harbor resentment and bitterness in my heart?
- Do I prioritize building a relationship with Jesus Christ as the foundation of my faith, seeking to walk in His footsteps and become more like Him each day, or do I treat Christianity as merely a set of beliefs or rituals to be observed?
- Am I cultivating a spirit of humility and teachability, recognizing that I am a work in progress and need God's grace and guidance, or am I prideful and resistant to correction or feedback from others?
- Do I prioritize building healthy boundaries in my relationships, respecting the autonomy and dignity of others while also asserting my needs and values, or do I engage in manipulation or coercion to control or manipulate others?
- Am I actively working to overcome prejudices or biases I may hold towards others based on their race, ethnicity, gender, sexual orientation, or socio-economic status, recognizing the inherent value and dignity of every human being as created in the image of God?
- Do I strive to live a life of authenticity and transparency, being honest and genuine in my interactions, or do I present a false image of myself to others out of fear or insecurity?
- Am I actively seeking to build bridges and foster understanding with those with different beliefs or perspectives than me, engaging in respectful dialogue and mutual learning, or do I engage in divisive rhetoric or hostility towards those who disagree with me?
- Do I practice self-care and prioritize my well-being, recognizing that I am a beloved child of God deserving of love and compassion, or do I neglect my needs and well-being in service to others to the point of burnout or exhaustion?
- Am I mindful of the impact of my words and actions on others, seeking to build up and encourage those around me, or do I engage in

gossip, slander, or hurtful speech that tears others down?

- Do I actively seek opportunities to serve and minister to those in need, recognizing the inherent dignity and worth of every person, or do I prioritize my comfort and convenience above the needs of others?
- Am I willing to confront injustice and speak truth to power, even when it is difficult or unpopular, or do I remain silent in the face of wrongdoing or oppression?
- Do I cultivate a spirit of gratitude and thanksgiving in all circumstances, recognizing God's goodness and faithfulness in my life, or do I complain or grumble when things do not go according to my plans?
- Am I actively seeking reconciliation and restoration in broken relationships, pursuing forgiveness and healing, or do I hold onto resentment and bitterness, allowing conflicts to fester and divide?
- Do I practice empathy and compassion towards those suffering or experiencing hardship, extending a listening ear and offering support, or do I remain indifferent or apathetic to the struggles of others?
- Am I committed to pursuing peace and reconciliation in all areas of my life, seeking to resolve conflicts and promote understanding, or do I contribute to discord and division through my words and actions?
- Do I steward my time, talents, and resources wisely, using them to glorify God and further His kingdom's purposes, or do I squander or misuse them for selfish gain or personal pleasure?
- Am I intentionally fostering a spirit of unity and cooperation within my Christian community, recognizing the diversity of gifts and perspectives, and working together for the common good, or do I contribute to division and disunity through gossip, criticism, or divisiveness?
- Do I actively seek opportunities for growth and learning in my faith journey, engaging in study, prayer, and spiritual disciplines, or do I become complacent or stagnant in my spiritual walk?
- Am I committed to living a life of integrity and honesty, aligning my actions with my beliefs and values, or do I compromise my principles or integrity for personal gain or acceptance by others?

- Do I practice gratitude and contentment in all circumstances, trusting in God's provision and faithfulness, or do I allow fear, worry, or discontentment to overshadow my faith?
- Am I willing to challenge cultural norms or societal injustices that conflict with biblical principles, advocating for righteousness and justice in the world around me, or do I conform to the patterns of this world?
- Do I cultivate a heart of worship and praise, recognizing God's sovereignty and majesty in all things, or do I allow distractions or idols to take precedence in my life?

Reflecting on these questions can help individuals evaluate their attitudes, actions, and priorities in light of their Christian faith. It's a journey of continual growth and transformation, guided by the principles of love, grace, and truth found in the teachings of Jesus Christ.

Fear And Projection

Fear Of Self-Examination And Projection Onto Others

The fear of self-examination and projection onto others is a psychological phenomenon whereby individuals, instead of introspectively confronting their flaws or insecurities, deflect attention away from themselves by attributing those characteristics to others. This concept explores the dynamics of fear, insecurity, and avoidance that underlie this behavior, examining how it manifests in interpersonal relationships, including within the context of religious belief systems like Christianity.

Understanding Projection

Psychological Defense Mechanism: Projection is a defense mechanism psychologists identify whereby individuals unconsciously attribute their undesirable thoughts, feelings, or traits to others.

Avoidance of Self-Awareness: Projection allows individuals to avoid confronting uncomfortable truths about themselves, such as insecurities, fears, or unresolved conflicts, by externalizing them onto others.

Distortion of Reality: Projection distorts individuals' perceptions of themselves and others, creating a skewed or distorted view of reality based on their internal struggles or conflicts.

Interplay with Fear: The fear of self-examination, often rooted in feelings of inadequacy, shame, or vulnerability, fuels the tendency to project onto others as a means of self-preservation.

Manifestations In Religious Contexts

Religious Hypocrisy: Within religious communities, individuals may project their moral failings or spiritual doubts onto others, criticizing or condemning them for behaviors or beliefs they struggle with.

Judgment and Condemnation: Fear of confronting one's imperfections may lead individuals to adopt a judgmental or self-righteous attitude toward others, using religious doctrine to justify their projection.

Scapegoating: In extreme cases, individuals may scapegoat marginalized groups or individuals, attributing their societal or personal anxieties to them and using religion as a tool to justify discrimination or persecution.

Institutional Dynamics: Religious institutions may inadvertently foster an environment where projection is encouraged or reinforced through authoritarian leadership, rigid dogma, or social hierarchies that discourage self-reflection and vulnerability.

Consequences Of Projection

Strained Relationships: Projection can strain interpersonal relationships, creating tension, resentment, and mistrust between individuals who perceive themselves as targets of projection and those engaging in projection.

Stagnation in Personal Growth: By deflecting responsibility onto others, individuals hinder their personal growth and development, perpetuating a cycle of avoidance and denial.

Erosion of Empathy: Projection diminishes individuals' capacity for empathy and understanding as they become more focused on externalizing their insecurities rather than empathizing with the experiences of others.

The undermining of Community Cohesion: Within religious communities, projection can undermine cohesion and unity, fostering division, conflict, and a lack of mutual support and compassion.

Addressing Projection

Cultivating Self-Awareness: Encouraging individuals to develop self-awareness through mindfulness, reflection, and therapy facilitates recognizing and acknowledging personal insecurities and fears.

Promoting Empathy: Fostering empathy and compassion within religious communities helps individuals better understand others' experiences and struggles, reducing the inclination to project onto them.

Creating Safe Spaces: Establishing safe spaces for open dialogue, vulnerability, and mutual support enables individuals to confront their fears and insecurities without fear of judgment or condemnation.

Encouraging Humility: Emphasizing humility as a core value in religious teachings encourages individuals to acknowledge their fallibility and imperfections, fostering a culture of accountability and self-reflection.

In summary, the fear of self-examination and projection onto others is a complex psychological phenomenon with profound implications for individual well-being and interpersonal relationships, including within religious contexts. By promoting self-awareness, empathy, and humility, individuals and communities can cultivate environments that encourage genuine introspection, mutual understanding, and authentic connection, fostering personal growth, compassion, and unity.

The Phenomenon Of Judgment As A Reflection Of Personal Insecurities

The phenomenon of judgment as a reflection of personal insecurities highlights how individuals may engage in critical or judgmental behavior towards others to cope with their insecurities, fears, or shortcomings. This concept delves into the psychological dynamics underlying judgmental attitudes, exploring how feelings of inadequacy or vulnerability manifest in outward criticism or condemnation of others.

Understanding Judgment As A Projection

Psychological Defense Mechanism: Judgment can function as a defense mechanism, allowing individuals to deflect attention away from their perceived inadequacies or vulnerabilities by focusing on the perceived faults or shortcomings of others.

Self-Preservation: By criticizing or condemning others, individuals may seek to elevate their sense of self-worth or competence, compensating for insecurity or inadequacy.

Distortion of Perception: Judgment distorts individuals' perceptions of themselves and others, projecting their internal struggles or insecurities onto those they judge, often exaggerating or magnifying perceived flaws.

The cycle of Negativity: Engaging in judgmental behavior perpetuates a cycle of negativity, reinforcing individuals' feelings of inadequacy while fostering resentment, mistrust, and division in relationships.

Manifestations In Social And Religious Contexts

Social Comparison: In social settings, individuals may judge others based on arbitrary criteria such as appearance, status, or achievement, using comparisons as a means of bolstering their self-esteem or sense of superiority.

Religious Judgment: Within religious communities, individuals may use moral or spiritual criteria to judge others' beliefs or behaviors, positioning themselves as arbiters of righteousness while struggling with their doubts, fears, or moral failings.

Scapegoating and Othering: In extreme cases, individuals may scapegoat marginalized groups or individuals, projecting their anxieties or insecurities onto them and using religion or ideology as a justification for discrimination or exclusion.

Rejection of Vulnerability: Judgmental attitudes may stem from a fear of vulnerability, as individuals seek to distance themselves from perceived weakness or imperfection by condemning those who embody traits or behaviors they associate with vulnerability.

Consequences Of Judgmental Behavior

Erosion of Empathy: Judgmental attitudes diminish individuals' capacity for empathy and understanding, as they become more focused on criticizing or condemning others rather than empathizing with their experiences or struggles.

Strained Relationships: Judgmental behavior can strain interpersonal relationships, creating tension, resentment, and mistrust between individuals who feel unfairly judged and those engaging in judgmental attitudes.

Stagnation in Personal Growth: By deflecting responsibility onto others, individuals hinder their personal growth and development, perpetuating a cycle of avoidance and denial.

The undermining of Community Cohesion: Within religious communities, judgmental attitudes can undermine cohesion and unity, fostering division, conflict, and a lack of mutual support and compassion.

Addressing Judgmental Attitudes

Cultivating Self-Awareness: Encouraging individuals to develop self-awareness through mindfulness, reflection, and therapy facilitates recognizing and acknowledging personal insecurities and fears.

Promoting Empathy: Fostering empathy and compassion within social and religious communities helps individuals better understand others' experiences and struggles, reducing the inclination to judge or condemn them.

Creating Safe Spaces: Establishing safe spaces for open dialogue, vulnerability, and mutual support enables individuals to confront their fears and insecurities without fear of judgment or condemnation.

Encouraging Humility: Emphasizing humility as a core value within social and religious contexts encourages individuals to acknowledge their fallibility and imperfections, fostering a culture of accountability and self-reflection.

In summary, judgment as a reflection of personal insecurities underscores the complex interplay between individual psychology, social dynamics, and relational well-being. By promoting self-awareness, empathy, and humility, individuals and communities can cultivate environments that encourage genuine introspection, mutual understanding, and authentic connection, fostering personal growth, compassion, and unity.

Analysis Of The Fear-Based Mindset In Religious Communities

Analysis of the fear-based mindset in religious communities involves examining how fear, often rooted in insecurity, uncertainty, or a desire for control, can shape individuals' beliefs, attitudes, and behaviors within religious contexts. This concept delves into the psychological, social, and theological dimensions of fear within spiritual communities, exploring its manifestations, consequences, and potential avenues for transformation.

Understanding The Fear-Based Mindset

Roots in Insecurity: Fear in religious communities often stems from insecurity or vulnerability, such as fear of divine judgment, uncertainty about salvation, or anxiety regarding one's spiritual standing.

Control and Certainty: Fear may arise from a desire for power or certainty in the face of existential questions, prompting individuals to cling to rigid beliefs or practices to ward off uncertainty or doubt.

Social Pressures: Fear can be perpetuated by social dynamics within religious communities, including pressure to conform, fear of ostracism or rejection, or the threat of punishment for deviating from established norms.

Authoritarian Leadership: Authoritarian leadership styles or hierarchical structures within religious institutions may cultivate a culture of fear, where individuals feel powerless or afraid to question authority or express dissenting views.

Theological Interpretations: Certain theological doctrines or interpretations may emphasize themes of fear, such as notions of divine wrath, eternal punishment, or the existential threat of spiritual adversaries, shaping individuals' perceptions of themselves, others, and the world.

Manifestations Of Fear In Religious Communities

Rigidity and Legalism: Fear-based mindsets may manifest in rigid adherence to religious laws or doctrines, focusing on rule-following and external conformity rather than inner transformation or spiritual growth.

Judgment and Condemnation: Fear can lead to judgmental attitudes towards others perceived as deviating from religious norms or beliefs, fostering a culture of exclusion, condemnation, or moral superiority.

Suppression of Doubt: Individuals may suppress doubts or questions out of fear of punishment or rejection, stifling intellectual curiosity or spiritual exploration and perpetuating a culture of intellectual stagnation.

Groupthink and Conformity: Fear-based mindsets may contribute to groupthink or conformity within religious communities, where individuals hesitate to challenge prevailing beliefs or practices for fear of social repercussions.

Us-vs-Them Mentality: Fear can foster an us-vs-them mentality, where individuals perceive outsiders or those with differing beliefs as threats to their identity or worldview, leading to polarization, conflict, or hostility.

Consequences Of Fear-Based Mindsets

Stifled Growth: Fear-based mindsets can inhibit personal and collective growth, hindering individuals' ability to question, learn, or evolve their beliefs and practices.

Diminished Empathy: Fear may erode empathy and compassion as individuals prioritize self-preservation or conformity over understanding and supporting others' experiences and struggles.

Social Division: Fear-based attitudes can fuel division, conflict, or hostility within religious communities, undermining cohesion, trust, and mutual respect.

Spiritual Stagnation: Individuals may become trapped in cycles of fear and anxiety, unable to experience the freedom, joy, and transformative power of authentic faith and spirituality.

Misrepresentation of Religion: Fear-based mindsets may distort or misrepresent the core values and teachings of religion, portraying faith as a source of fear or oppression rather than liberation, love, and reconciliation.

Transforming Fear Into Love And Empowerment

Cultivating Awareness: Encouraging individuals to develop awareness of their fears and insecurities, fostering an environment of honesty, vulnerability, and support within religious communities.

Promoting Critical Thinking: Emphasizing critical thinking and intellectual inquiry, encouraging individuals to engage with religious teachings and doctrines thoughtfully and discerningly.

Fostering Empathy: Cultivating empathy and compassion, fostering a sense of interconnectedness and solidarity that transcends religious, cultural, or ideological boundaries.

Empowering Authenticity: Empowering individuals to embrace authenticity, courageously confronting their doubts, fears, and vulnerabilities, and embracing the transformative power of vulnerability and self-acceptance.

Reimagining Theology: Reimagining theological interpretations to emphasize themes of love, grace, and liberation, reframing religious narratives to inspire hope, inclusion, and empowerment.

Analyzing fear-based mindsets in religious communities illuminates the complex interplay between psychology, theology, and social dynamics in shaping individuals' beliefs, attitudes, and behaviors. By confronting fear with awareness, empathy, and authenticity, religious communities can cultivate environments that foster growth, compassion, and spiritual liberation, transforming fear into love, empowerment, and a deeper connection with the divine.

Ask Yourself If You Are Projecting Your Fears.

Reflecting on whether we are projecting our fears onto others is essential to self-awareness and emotional intelligence. Projection is a psychological defense mechanism where individuals attribute unacceptable or unwanted thoughts, feelings, or impulses to others, often without conscious awareness. Asking ourselves if we are projecting our fears involves examining our thoughts, behaviors, and interactions with others to identify any projection patterns.

Here are some considerations to delve deeper into this question:

Awareness of Fear Triggers: Take note of situations or interactions that elicit strong emotional reactions or trigger feelings of discomfort or insecurity. These may be indicators of underlying fears that are being projected onto others.

Examination of Reactions: Pay attention to how you react to certain behaviors or characteristics in others. Are there specific traits or behaviors that consistently evoke strong adverse reactions from you? These could reflect fears or insecurities within yourself that you are projecting onto others.

Exploration of Past Experiences: Reflect on past experiences or relationships where projection may have occurred. Consider whether you attribute negative qualities or intentions to others based on your unresolved issues or past traumas.

Honest Self-Reflection: Engage in honest self-reflection to identify and acknowledge your fears, insecurities, and vulnerabilities. This may involve journaling, therapy, or conversations with trusted friends or mentors to gain deeper insight into your inner world.

Empathy and Perspective-Taking: Practice empathy and perspective-taking by considering the thoughts, feelings, and experiences of others. Recognize that everyone has fears and insecurities, and try to approach interactions with compassion and understanding.

Mindfulness Practices: Incorporate mindfulness into your daily routine to cultivate present-moment awareness and observe your thoughts and emotions without judgment. This can help you become more attuned to any tendencies toward projection.

Seeking Feedback: Be open to receiving feedback from others about your behavior and interactions. Trusted friends or family members can offer valuable insights and observations that may shed light on any projection patterns.

Commitment to Growth: Commit to personal growth and self-improvement by actively addressing and processing your fears and insecurities. This may involve seeking therapy, practicing self-compassion, and challenging negative thought patterns.

Recognizing Patterns of Blame: Pay attention to whether you blame others for situations or outcomes that your fears or insecurities may influence. Projection often involves shifting responsibility onto others to avoid confronting uncomfortable truths about ourselves.

Exploring Triggers in Relationships: Reflect on how your fears may impact your relationships with others, particularly in conflict or tension. Consider whether certain behaviors or traits in others trigger defensive reactions from you, signaling potential areas of projection.

Examining Communication Dynamics: Evaluate how you communicate with others, particularly during disagreements or misunderstandings. Notice if you attribute negative motives or intentions to others without considering alternative perspectives, which can indicate projection.

Understanding Projection in Group Settings: Consider how projection may manifest in group dynamics, such as scapegoating or attributing collective anxieties or fears to specific individuals or groups. Awareness of these dynamics can help mitigate the harmful effects of projection within communities.

Differentiating Projection from Intuition: Distinguish between genuine intuition or discernment and projection. While intuition may offer valuable insights into situations or people, projection distorts perception. It is rooted in personal fears or biases.

Cultivating Emotional Regulation: Practice techniques for managing and regulating emotions, such as deep breathing, mindfulness meditation, or grounding exercises. Developing emotional resilience can reduce the likelihood of projecting fears onto others in stressful or challenging situations.

Seeking Feedback and Validation: Engage in open and honest conversations with trusted individuals who can provide constructive feedback and validation. They can help you identify blind spots or patterns of projection that may be impacting your relationships and interactions.

Accountability and ership: Take responsibility for your thoughts, feelings, and actions, even when they may be uncomfortable or challenging to acknowledge. Recognize that projection is a defense mechanism that protects the ego but ultimately hinders personal growth and connection with others.

Practicing Empathy and Compassion: Cultivate empathy and compassion towards yourself and others, recognizing that we are all navigating complex inner worlds shaped by past experiences and conditioning. Approach interactions with curiosity and a genuine desire to understand the perspectives of others.

Reflecting on Cultural and Societal Influences: Consider how cultural norms, societal expectations, and media portrayals may contribute to internalizing and projecting fears and insecurities. Questioning and challenging these influences can lead to greater self-awareness and authenticity.

Analyzing Defensive Responses: Pay attention to defensive reactions or deflections in conversations or situations touching sensitive topics. These responses can indicate projection, as individuals may seek to protect themselves from confronting their fears or insecurities.

Reflecting on Personal Triggers: Identify specific triggers or situations that provoke strong emotional reactions within yourself. These triggers may reveal underlying fears or unresolved issues that are being projected onto others.

Examining Perceptions of Others: Take a closer look at how you perceive and judge the actions, behaviors, and intentions of others. Are you quick to attribute negative motives or assume the worst about their intentions? This tendency could be a sign of projection.

Considering Cultural and Familial Influences: Reflect on how your upbringing and cultural background may have shaped your beliefs, values, and fears. Family dynamics and societal norms can contribute to developing projection patterns that persist into adulthood.

Practicing Vulnerability and Authenticity: Embrace vulnerability and authenticity in your relationships by openly acknowledging and expressing your fears and insecurities. Creating a safe space for honesty and transparency can encourage others to do the same, fostering deeper connections and understanding.

Seeking Support and Guidance: Contact trusted friends, family members, or mentors to navigate your fears and projections. Sometimes, an outside perspective can offer valuable insights and help you clarify challenging situations.

Engaging in Self-Compassion: Practice self-compassion and self-care as you explore and address your fears and insecurities. Treat yourself with kindness and understanding, recognizing that facing these challenges is a courageous and essential step in personal growth.

Challenging Assumptions and Biases: Challenge assumptions and biases that may underlie your projections of others. Be willing to question your perspectives and consider alternative interpretations of events or behaviors.

Learning from Past Patterns: Reflect on past experiences where projection may have played a role in your interactions or relationships. What patterns or themes emerge? What lessons can you learn from these experiences to help you navigate similar situations in the future?

Committing to Growth and Healing: Commit to ongoing growth and healing as you work to address your fears and projections. This journey may involve therapy, self-reflection, spiritual practices, and other tools for personal development.

By exploring these additional considerations, you can deepen your understanding of how projection may manifest in your life and relationships and take proactive steps toward greater self-awareness and emotional well-being.

Misinterpretation And Blind Faith

High IQ Interpretation vs. Blind Following Of False Prophets

The dichotomy between high IQ interpretation and blind following of false prophets within religious contexts underscores the complex interplay between intelligence, critical thinking, and belief systems. This concept explores the tension between intellectual discernment and uncritical adherence to charismatic leaders or ideological frameworks, examining how individuals navigate religious beliefs, authority, and skepticism in the pursuit of truth and authenticity.

High IQ Interpretation

Critical Thinking: High IQ interpretation emphasizes essential thinking skills, analytical reasoning, and intellectual curiosity in evaluating religious teachings, doctrines, and practices.

Questioning Authority: Individuals engage in independent inquiry and reflection, questioning religious authorities, texts, or traditions to discern the validity and relevance of their beliefs in light of evidence, reason, and personal experience.

Openness to Diversity: High IQ interpretation encourages openness to diverse perspectives, interpretations, and sources of knowledge, recognizing the complexity and nuance of religious and philosophical discourse.

Integration of Knowledge: Individuals draw upon various disciplines, including theology, philosophy, science, and history, to inform their understanding of religious concepts, values, and ethics.

Blind Following of False Prophets

Charismatic Influence: Blindly following false prophets often involves uncritical acceptance of charismatic leaders or authorities who claim unique insight or divine authority without questioning their motives, teachings, or behavior.

Lack of Discernment: Individuals may prioritize emotional or psychological factors over intellectual discernment, seeking comfort, security, or belonging in the charismatic appeal of false prophets rather than critically evaluating their claims or teachings.

Groupthink and Conformity: Blind followers may succumb to groupthink or social pressure within religious communities, suppressing dissenting voices or alternative viewpoints that challenge the authority or legitimacy of false prophets.

Manipulation and Exploitation: False prophets may exploit their followers' trust and vulnerability for personal gain, exerting control, extracting resources, or perpetuating harmful ideologies under the guise of religious authority.

Navigating the Dichotomy

Promoting Critical Literacy: Encouraging individuals to develop critical literacy skills, including media literacy, theological literacy, and philosophical literacy, to navigate religious discourse and discern truth from falsehood.

Fostering Skepticism: Cultivating a healthy skepticism and willingness to question authority, inviting individuals to challenge religious dogma, tradition, or leaders when inconsistencies, contradictions, or ethical concerns arise.

Empowering Autonomy: Empowering individuals to cultivate autonomy and agency in their religious beliefs and practices, fostering a sense of personal responsibility and accountability for their spiritual journey.

Building Resilience: Equipping individuals with emotional resilience and psychological fortitude to withstand manipulation, coercion, or undue influence from charismatic leaders or false prophets.

Encouraging Pluralism: Embracing religious pluralism and interfaith dialogue, fostering mutual respect, understanding, and cooperation among individuals of diverse religious backgrounds and beliefs.

In summary, the dichotomy between high IQ interpretation and blind following of false prophets highlights the importance of critical thinking, discernment, and ethical integrity in navigating religious beliefs and authority. By fostering intellectual curiosity, skepticism, and openness to diverse perspectives, religious communities can cultivate environments that empower individuals to engage authentically with their faith, resist manipulation and exploitation, and pursue truth, meaning, and spiritual fulfillment with clarity and integrity.

Examination Of The Role Of Critical Thinking In Religious Interpretation

The examination of the role of critical thinking in religious interpretation explores how individuals engage with religious texts, beliefs, and practices through the lens of analytical reasoning, skepticism, and intellectual inquiry. This concept delves into the significance of critical thinking in navigating the complexities of religious discourse, fostering personal growth, ethical discernment, and authentic engagement with faith.

Foundations of Critical Thinking

Analytical Skills: Critical thinking in religious interpretation involves the application of analytical skills such as logic, reasoning, and evidence evaluation to examine religious texts, doctrines, and teachings.

Skepticism and Inquiry: Individuals approach religious beliefs with healthy skepticism, questioning assumptions, assertions, and dogma to discern truth from falsehood and engage with faith in an intellectually honest and responsible manner.

Open-Mindedness: Critical thinkers maintain an open-minded attitude towards religious diversity, alternative interpretations, and new perspectives, recognizing the multifaceted nature of spiritual truth and the limitations of their understanding.

Integration of Knowledge: Critical thinkers draw upon diverse disciplines such as theology, philosophy, history, and science to enrich their understanding of religious concepts, values, and ethical principles, integrating insights from multiple sources into their interpretation.

Applications in Religious Interpretation

Textual Analysis: Critical thinking informs textual analysis of religious scriptures, guiding individuals to examine historical context, linguistic nuances,

Social Conditioning: Cultural or societal norms within religious communities may promote blind faith as a virtue, equating skepticism or questioning with moral weakness or spiritual deficiency.

Consequences of Blind Faith

Hate Speech and Violence: Blind faith can contribute to the spread of hate speech and violence against marginalized groups, as individuals justify discriminatory attitudes or actions based on religious beliefs or interpretations.

Exclusion and Marginalization: Blind faith may lead to the exclusion or marginalization of individuals who do not conform to religious norms or standards, perpetuating social divisions and inequalities within religious communities.

Justification of Discrimination: Blind faith may serve as a justification for discrimination or oppression against certain groups, as individuals invoke religious doctrines or teachings to rationalize their prejudiced attitudes or behaviors.

Inhibition of Social Progress: Blind faith can inhibit social progress by resisting change or reform efforts that challenge entrenched religious beliefs or practices, perpetuating injustices and inequalities that impede societal advancement.

Undermining Human Rights: Blind faith may undermine human rights by prioritizing religious doctrine or authority over principles of equality, dignity, and freedom, legitimizing violations of individual rights or liberties in the name of religious tradition or orthodoxy.

Addressing Blind Faith

Promoting Critical Thinking: Encouraging critical thinking and intellectual inquiry within religious communities fosters a culture of openness, dialogue, and reflection that challenges blind faith and promotes a deeper understanding of spiritual teachings and values.

Emphasizing Compassion and Empathy: Emphasizing compassion and empathy in religious teachings cultivates a sense of solidarity and mutual respect that transcends religious differences, fostering a more inclusive and tolerant society.

Advocating for Social Justice: Advocating for social justice and human rights within religious communities challenges discriminatory attitudes and behaviors that arise from blind faith, promoting equality, fairness, and dignity for all individuals.

Fostering Interfaith Dialogue: Fostering interfaith dialogue and cooperation promotes understanding and collaboration among individuals of different religious backgrounds, challenging stereotypes and prejudices that fuel hate and discrimination.

Empowering Individuals: Empowering individuals to question religious authority and dogma and assert their agency and autonomy in faith cultivates a culture of accountability and personal responsibility that mitigates the harmful consequences of blind faith.

In summary, the consequences of blind faith, when coupled with intolerance or prejudice, can perpetuate hate and discrimination within religious communities and society at large. By promoting critical thinking, compassion, and social justice, spiritual communities can counteract the harmful effects of blind faith, fostering a culture of inclusivity, tolerance, and respect that honors the dignity and humanity of all individuals, regardless of their religious beliefs or backgrounds.

Have You Made Your Decisions About Your Beliefs, Or Are You Following Someone Else's?

Asking oneself whether they have made decisions about one's beliefs or simply following someone else's beliefs is a fundamental aspect of self-awareness and autonomy in faith and personal conviction. It prompts individuals to critically evaluate the origins and foundations of their beliefs, considering whether they have been shaped by independent thought and personal exploration or if they have been adopted unquestioningly from external sources.

Here are some points to consider when exploring this question:

Reflecting on Influences: Take stock of the influences that have shaped your beliefs, including family, culture, religious institutions, and influential figures.

Consider how these influences have impacted the formation of your worldview and values.

Examining the Basis of Beliefs: Evaluate the reasons behind your beliefs and convictions. Have you thoroughly reviewed and evaluated the evidence and arguments for your beliefs, or have you accepted them without critical scrutiny?

Assessing Intellectual Independence: Consider whether you have actively engaged in critical thinking and intellectual inquiry to arrive at your conclusions or if you have relied on the authority or guidance of others to shape your beliefs.

Exploring Personal Experience: Reflect on your lived experiences and how they have influenced your beliefs. Have personal experiences significantly shaped your worldview and spiritual beliefs, or have you primarily relied on external sources of authority?

Questioning Assumptions: Challenge any assumptions or presuppositions that underlie your beliefs. Are there aspects of your beliefs you have taken for granted without questioning or examining them critically?

Seeking Authenticity: Strive to align your beliefs with your authentic self and values rather than conforming to external expectations or pressures. Consider whether your beliefs resonate with your deepest convictions and aspirations.

Embracing Growth and Change: Remain open to growth and evolution in your beliefs over time. Recognize that beliefs are not static and may evolve as you gain new insights, experiences, and perspectives.

Cultivating Discernment: Develop the ability to discern between genuine convictions rooted in personal reflection and discernment and beliefs adopted uncritically or without thoughtful consideration.

Honoring Diversity of Belief: Respect the diversity of beliefs and perspectives held by others, recognizing that each individual's journey of faith and religion is unique and deserving of respect.

Exploring Personal Values: Reflect on your core values and principles and how they align with your beliefs. Are your beliefs consistent with your values, or do you find discrepancies between what you believe and what you truly value?

Assessing Emotional Influence: Consider the role of emotions in shaping your beliefs. Have your feelings, such as fear, guilt, or desire for belonging, influenced your beliefs, or have you approached your beliefs with emotional resilience and rationality?

Examining Authority Figures: Evaluate the authority figures or sources of influence in your life and how they have impacted your beliefs. Have you critically evaluated their teachings and perspectives, or have you passively accepted them without question?

Understanding Group Dynamics: Reflect on the influence of group dynamics on your beliefs. Have you adopted certain beliefs because they are socially or culturally acceptable within your community, or have you dared to challenge the status quo and think independently?

Considering Education and Exposure: Assess the role of education and exposure to diverse perspectives in shaping your beliefs. Have you actively sought new knowledge and different viewpoints or remained within a narrow echo chamber of familiar ideas?

Recognizing Cognitive Biases: Be mindful of cognitive biases that may cloud your judgment and reasoning when forming beliefs. Are you susceptible to confirmation bias, where you seek out information that confirms your preexisting beliefs, or do you actively seek evidence that challenges your beliefs?

Embracing Personal Responsibility: Take ownership of your beliefs and the decisions that have led you to them. Are you willing to take responsibility for your beliefs, even if they are unpopular or divergent from the mainstream?

Seeking Authenticity: Strive to cultivate authenticity and integrity in your beliefs, aligning them with your true self and inner convictions. Are your beliefs genuinely reflecting who you are, or are they façade adopted to please others or fit in with a specific group?

Promoting Open Dialogue: Foster open dialogue and respectful discourse with others about your beliefs. Are you open to constructive conversations with people with different beliefs, or do you shy away from challenging discussions?

Assessing Personal Experience: Reflect on how your personal experiences have shaped your beliefs. Have significant life events or encounters influenced the development of your worldview and spiritual convictions?

Evaluating Consistency: Consider the consistency and coherence of your beliefs across different aspects of life. Do your beliefs align with your moral principles, ethical standards, and behavior in various contexts?

Examining Cultural Influences: Explore the impact of cultural norms, traditions, and societal expectations on your beliefs. Does cultural conditioning influence your beliefs, and if so, how do you navigate between cultural influences and personal convictions?

Reflecting on Spiritual Journey: Trace the evolution of your beliefs over time and across different stages of your spiritual journey. How have your beliefs evolved or deepened as you've matured or encountered new perspectives?

Engaging with Sacred Texts: Examine your interpretation and understanding of sacred texts or teachings within your faith tradition. Does a critical engagement with religious texts inform your beliefs, or do you rely solely on interpretations handed out by others?

Considering Moral Reasoning: Reflect on the moral reasoning underlying your beliefs. Do you prioritize ethical considerations and moral principles when forming beliefs, or are your beliefs primarily shaped by dogma or doctrinal adherence?

Exploring Intellectual Curiosity: Cultivate intellectual curiosity and a thirst for knowledge in exploring your beliefs. Are you open to questioning and challenging your beliefs, or do you resist new information or perspectives that may challenge your worldview?

Seeking Spiritual Guidance: Seek spiritual guidance and mentorship from individuals who embody wisdom and integrity in their beliefs. Are you open to learning from others who have walked a similar path or have valuable insights to offer?

Practicing Discernment: Develop discernment in discerning truth from falsehood, wisdom from folly, and genuine spiritual insight from mere rhetoric or manipulation. Are you discerning when evaluating the authenticity and sincerity of spiritual teachings and leaders?

Cultivating Gratitude: Cultivate gratitude for the freedom and opportunity to explore and shape your beliefs. Are you grateful for diverse perspectives and experiences that enrich your spiritual journey and contribute to your growth and understanding?

By exploring these additional considerations, individuals can deepen their self-awareness and discernment in discerning the origins and authenticity of their beliefs. This introspective inquiry empowers individuals to take ownership of their spiritual journey and embrace a more authentic and meaningful expression of their beliefs.

Misinterpretation and blind faith are interconnected concepts that can lead to misunderstandings, misconceptions, and potentially harmful outcomes, especially within religious contexts. Let's explore these concepts in more detail:

Misinterpretation

Misinterpretation refers to the incorrect understanding or interpretation of religious texts, teachings, or doctrines. This can occur due to various factors:

Lack of Context: Misinterpreting passages without considering their historical, cultural, or linguistic context can lead to erroneous conclusions.

Personal Bias: Individuals may interpret religious teachings based on preconceived notions, biases, or cultural influences.

Selective Reading: Cherry-picking verses or passages without considering the broader context of the religious text can result in distorted interpretations.

Literalism: Taking religious texts too literally without considering metaphorical or symbolic meanings can lead to misunderstandings.

Consequences of Misinterpretation

Misinterpretation can have significant consequences, including:

Conflict: Misinterpretations of religious teachings can lead to doctrinal disputes, schisms, or conflicts within religious communities.

Misguided Practices: Incorrect interpretations may lead to adopting practices or beliefs that are not aligned with the original intent of the religion.

Harmful Behaviors: Misinterpretations can justify harmful behaviors or attitudes towards others, such as discrimination, intolerance, or violence.

Stagnation: Misinterpretations may hinder personal or spiritual growth by promoting narrow-mindedness or rigidity in belief systems.

Blind Faith

Blind faith refers to unquestioning belief or acceptance of religious teachings or doctrines without critical examination or inquiry. This can stem from:

Authority Figures: Individuals may blindly follow religious leaders or authorities without questioning their teachings or actions.

Cultural Conditioning: Cultural norms or societal pressure may encourage blind adherence to religious beliefs without thoughtful consideration.

Fear of Doubt: Fear of doubt or uncertainty may lead individuals to cling to beliefs without seeking deeper understanding or clarification.

Emotional Comfort: Belief in religious doctrines may provide emotional comfort or security, leading individuals to avoid challenging their faith.

Consequences of Blind Faith

Blind faith can have both positive and negative consequences:

Positive: Blind faith can provide solace, hope, and a sense of purpose to individuals facing adversity or uncertainty.

Negative: Blind faith may lead to intellectual stagnation, intolerance towards differing beliefs, or susceptibility to manipulation by unscrupulous leaders.

Overcoming Misinterpretation and Blind Faith

Overcoming misinterpretation and blind faith requires critical thinking, open-mindedness, and a willingness to engage in self-reflection:

Critical Analysis: Critically analyze religious texts, teachings, and beliefs, considering multiple perspectives and interpretations.

Seeking Knowledge: Educate oneself about religious texts' historical, cultural, and linguistic contexts to understand their meanings.

Questioning Authority: Questioning religious authorities or leaders when their teachings or actions seem contradictory or harmful.

Personal Reflection: Reflect on one's beliefs and values, discerning whether they align with the core principles of one's faith and promoting personal growth and spiritual development.

Importance of Discernment

Discernment plays a crucial role in navigating religious beliefs and practices:

Balance: Strive for a balance between faith and critical inquiry, avoiding extremes of blind adherence or skepticism.

Humility: Recognize the limitations of human understanding and approach religious beliefs with humility and openness to new insights.

Ethical Considerations: Consider the ethical and moral implications of one's beliefs and actions, ensuring they promote compassion, justice, and respect for others.

In summary, misinterpretation and blind faith can hinder authentic spiritual growth and understanding within religious communities. By fostering critical thinking, seeking knowledge, and promoting open dialogue, individuals can overcome misconceptions and cultivate a deeper, more nuanced understanding of their faith. This approach encourages personal growth, fosters mutual respect and learning, and promotes the positive aspects of religious belief while mitigating the potential harms associated with misinterpretation and blind faith.

Quoting The Bible Without Reading It Or Understanding It

Superficial Knowledge: Understanding the Bible in Depth

The Pitfalls of Superficial Knowledge

Quoting the Bible without a thorough reading or understanding often results in a superficial grasp of its messages. This superficiality can lead to misinterpretation and misuse of biblical texts, failing to capture their intended depth and meaning. The Bible is a complex and nuanced text, rich in historical, cultural, and theological context. Without this depth of knowledge, one's understanding remains shallow and potentially misleading.

Why Superficial Knowledge is Problematic

Contextual Ignorance: The Bible contains texts written in various historical and cultural contexts. Ignoring these contexts can lead to incorrect interpretations. For example, some verses might address specific situations or practices of ancient communities that do not directly apply to modern life without careful interpretation.

Cherry-Picking: Selectively quoting verses without understanding their broader context can distort their meaning. This practice, often called cherry-picking, can support preconceived notions rather than the holistic message of the scripture.

Theological Inaccuracy

Doctrinal Errors: A superficial understanding can lead to incorrect theological conclusions. For instance, taking a verse literally without understanding its symbolic or metaphorical meaning might result in doctrinal inaccuracies.

Incomplete Messages: The Bible's teachings are interconnected. Isolating verses can result in incomplete or skewed messages, missing the comprehensive nature of biblical doctrine.

Harmful Applications

Justifying Misconduct: Misinterpreted scriptures have been used historically to justify harmful behaviors and policies, such as slavery, discrimination, and violence. Without proper understanding, the Bible can be misused to endorse actions contrary to its core message of love and justice.

Spiritual Confusion: Superficial knowledge can lead to confusion and doubt among believers. Misleading interpretations might cause people to question their faith or abandon it altogether due to perceived contradictions or harsh teachings.

Importance of In-Depth Understanding

Historical and Cultural Context

Contextual Analysis: Understanding biblical texts' historical and cultural backdrop is crucial. For example, many of Jesus' parables are deeply rooted in the agricultural society of his time. Recognizing this context helps modern readers grasp the intended lessons.

Archaeological Insights: Archaeological findings and historical research provide valuable insights into biblical times, enhancing comprehension of various passages.

Literary Forms and Genres

Recognizing Genres: The Bible contains diverse literary forms, including poetry, prophecy, narrative, and epistles. Each genre requires a different approach to interpretation. For instance, poetic books like Psalms use metaphorical language that should not always be taken literally.

Literary Techniques: Understanding literary devices such as symbolism, hyperbole, and parables is essential for interpreting the Bible accurately. These techniques often convey deeper spiritual truths.

Theological Framework

Doctrinal Consistency: A thorough understanding ensures that individual interpretations align with the overall theological framework of the Bible. This consistency helps in forming a coherent belief system.

Systematic Theology: Studying systematic theology, which organizes biblical teachings into coherent doctrines, can provide a structured understanding of key themes such as salvation, grace, and eschatology.

Spiritual Growth

Deepening Faith: In-depth study fosters a deeper, more mature faith. Understanding the complexities and nuances of the Bible strengthens believers' relationship with God and their confidence in their faith.

Personal Transformation: The Bible's transformative power is fully realized when its teachings are understood and applied correctly. Deep knowledge encourages personal growth and ethical living according to biblical principles.

Steps to Achieve In-Depth Understanding

Comprehensive Reading

Systematic Study: Engage in systematic reading plans that cover the entire Bible. This approach prevents selective reading and encourages understanding the Bible's comprehensive message.

Multiple Translations: Reading different translations can provide varied perspectives and enhance understanding of difficult passages.

Study Tools and Resources

Commentaries and Study Bibles: Utilize scholarly commentaries and study Bibles that provide historical, cultural, and theological insights. These resources can clarify difficult passages and offer a more profound understanding.

Original Languages: Learning the basics of biblical Hebrew and Greek can provide richer insights into the original meanings of the texts.

Community and Discussion

Study Groups: Participating in Bible study groups fosters communal learning and allows for diverse perspectives. Group discussions can challenge superficial interpretations and encourage more profound analysis.

Mentorship: Seeking guidance from knowledgeable mentors or religious leaders can provide personalized insights and support in understanding complex theological concepts.

Prayer and Meditation

Spiritual Reflection: Regular prayer and meditation on the scriptures invite the Holy Spirit to guide understanding and reveal more profound truths. Reflective practices help internalize and apply biblical teachings.

Theological Education

Formal Studies: Enrolling in theological courses or attending seminary can provide structured and in-depth biblical education. These programs often cover critical aspects of biblical studies, including exegesis, hermeneutics, and church history.

In summary, a superficial knowledge of the Bible can lead to misinterpretations and misapplications of its teachings. To grasp its messages, one must delve into its historical, cultural, and theological depths. By engaging in comprehensive reading, using study tools, participating in community discussions, and seeking spiritual guidance, believers can achieve a deeper and more accurate understanding of the Bible, enriching their faith and guiding their lives more faithfully according to its principles.

Misinterpretation

Misinterpreting biblical verses is a common challenge when individuals lack a comprehensive understanding of the text. Context plays a crucial role in interpreting Scripture accurately. Here's a closer look at the factors contributing to misinterpretation and the importance of context:

Lack of Comprehensive Understanding

Misinterpretation often occurs when individuals approach the Bible with limited knowledge of its historical, cultural, and linguistic context.

Without a deep understanding of the broader themes, motifs, and literary styles present in the Bible, readers may misconstrue the intended meaning of specific verses.

Risk of Taking Verses out of Context

Many verses can be quickly taken out of context, leading to misunderstandings about the Bible's teachings.

Pulling a verse from its surrounding passages or historical context can distort its original meaning and misrepresent the author's intentions.

Importance of Historical and Cultural Background

Understanding a passage's historical and cultural background is essential for grasping its meaning.

The Bible was written in specific historical contexts, addressing ancient communities' concerns, beliefs, and practices. Modern readers may misinterpret the significance of certain events or teachings without this background knowledge.

Interpretive Methods and Approaches

Different interpretive methods, such as literalism, allegory, or historical-critical analysis, can lead to varying interpretations of the exact text.

Readers may impose their biases, preferences, or preconceived notions onto the text, shaping their interpretation according to personal beliefs rather than the text's intended meaning.

Role of Translation and Language

Translating ancient texts into modern languages introduces additional challenges, as nuances, idioms, and cultural references may be lost or distorted.

The original languages of the Bible, such as Hebrew, Greek, and Aramaic, contain layers of meaning that may not fully translate into English or other modern languages.

In summary, misinterpreting biblical verses can lead to confusion, misrepresentation, and even theological error. To mitigate this risk, readers should approach the Bible with humility, openness, and a willingness to engage deeply with its historical, cultural, and linguistic contexts. Consulting reputable commentaries, studying the original languages, and engaging in thoughtful dialogue with other believers can also help clarify and deepen understanding of the Scriptures. Ultimately, a nuanced and contextual approach to interpretation is essential for uncovering the richness and depth of the Bible's teachings.

Manipulation

Manipulation of Scripture occurs when individuals quote the Bible without a thorough understanding, often to serve personal biases or agendas. Here's a deeper exploration of this issue:

Cherry-Picking Verses

Manipulation of Scripture often involves cherry-picking verses that align with preconceived beliefs or desired outcomes.

Individuals can distort the passage's intended meaning by selecting verses out of context and using them to support their viewpoints while ignoring the broader context or contradictory passages.

Ignoring Broader Principles

Manipulators may focus solely on isolated verses that support their agenda while disregarding broader biblical principles that provide balance and deeper insight.

This selective approach fails to consider the holistic message of the Bible, leading to a shallow understanding of its teachings and ethical principles.

Justifying Personal Biases

Individuals may manipulate Scripture to justify their personal biases, prejudices, or discriminatory attitudes.

By misinterpreting or misrepresenting biblical passages, manipulators can perpetuate harmful beliefs or behaviors under the guise of religious authority.

Promoting Agenda-driven Interpretations

Manipulators may twist the meaning of Scripture to promote a specific agenda or political ideology.

This instrumental use of the Bible undermines its sacredness and integrity, reducing it to a tool for advancing personal or group interests rather than a guide for spiritual truth and moral guidance.

Misrepresentation and Deception

Manipulation of Scripture involves misrepresentation and deception, as individuals distort the meaning of biblical texts to serve their ends.

This can lead to confusion, mistrust, and harm within religious communities, as false interpretations and misapplications of Scripture mislead people.

Guarding Against Manipulation

To guard against manipulating Scripture, approaching the Bible with humility, honesty, and a commitment to understanding its context and overarching message is essential.

Engaging in thorough study, consulting reputable commentaries, and seeking guidance from trusted spiritual mentors can help discern the true meaning of Scripture and guard against manipulation and misuse.

In summary, the manipulation of Scripture undermines its authority. It distorts its message, leading to confusion, division, and harm within religious communities. By promoting a deeper understanding of the Bible's teachings, fostering discernment, and encouraging humility in interpretation, individuals can guard against manipulation and uphold the integrity of Scripture as a source of spiritual truth and moral guidance.

Lack of Authenticity

Lack of authenticity in quoting the Bible occurs when individuals do so without a genuine understanding of its message. Here's a closer look at this issue:

Superficial Engagement

Quoting the Bible without genuine understanding often stems from a superficial engagement with the text.

Rather than profoundly studying and reflecting on its messages, individuals may repeat verses they have heard without internalizing their significance or relevance to their lives.

Shallow Knowledge

Lack of authenticity in quoting the Bible may indicate a shallow knowledge of its contents and teachings.

Without investing time and effort in studying Scripture, individuals may struggle to grasp the nuanced meanings and contexts of the verses they quote, leading to superficial interpretations.

Hypocrisy and Insincerity

Inauthentic quoting of the Bible can be perceived as hypocritical or insincere, especially if it contradicts one's actions or beliefs.

People may use biblical quotes to project a specific image of purity or righteousness without genuinely embodying the values and principles espoused by the scriptures.

Undermining Credibility

Quoting the Bible without understanding can undermine credibility and authority as a spokesperson for Christian beliefs.

Without a solid foundation of knowledge and comprehension, individuals may struggle to articulate the deeper truths and insights of Scripture, leading to skepticism or dismissal by others.

Perceived Lack of Integrity

Lack of authenticity in quoting the Bible can erode trust and integrity within religious communities.

When people sense that others are quoting Scripture for show or to manipulate rather than out of genuine conviction or understanding, it can breed cynicism and skepticism about the sincerity of their faith.

Cultivating Authentic Engagement

Authentic engagement with Scripture requires a sincere effort to study, reflect, and comprehend its messages.

Individuals can deepen their understanding and authenticity by quoting the Bible, cultivating a habit of prayerful reading, seeking guidance from knowledgeable mentors, and applying biblical teachings to one's lives.

In summary, inauthentic quoting of the Bible reflects a lack of genuine engagement with its message and undermines the credibility and sincerity of one's faith. By prioritizing authentic study, reflection, and application of Scripture, individuals can cultivate a deeper understanding and appreciation of its teachings, leading to more genuine expressions of faith and a more impactful witness to others.

Failure To Embody Teachings

Failure to embody the teachings of the Bible involves a disconnect between quoting Scripture and living out its principles in daily life. Here's a deeper exploration of this issue:

Superficial Application

Merely quoting Scripture without embodying its teachings - often results in a superficial application of biblical principles.

While individuals may recite verses, they may fail to integrate these teachings into their attitudes, behaviors, and relationships.

Lack of Internalization

Without genuine understanding, it's challenging to internalize and practice biblical values.

Quoting Scripture without comprehension may lead to a shallow grasp of its significance, making it difficult for individuals to apply its teachings authentically.

Hypocrisy and Inconsistency

Failure to embody the teachings of the Bible can result in hypocrisy and inconsistency in one's faith.

People may profess certain beliefs or values based on Scripture but fail to live them out consistently in their actions, leading to a disconnect between their words and deeds.

Diminished Impact

When individuals fail to embody the teachings of the Bible, it diminishes the impact of their witness and testimony.

Others may be skeptical or dismissive of their faith if they perceive a discrepancy between what they preach and how they live, undermining the credibility of their message.

Missed Opportunities for Transformation

Genuine transformation occurs when individuals internalize and practice the teachings of the Bible in their daily lives.

Failure to embody these teachings represents a missed opportunity for personal growth, spiritual maturity, and positive impact on others.

Cultivating Authentic Living

Cultivating authentic living requires intentional effort to align one's beliefs, values, and actions with the teachings of the Bible.

This involves regular self-examination, prayerful reflection, and a commitment to living out biblical principles in all areas of life.

In summary, failure to embody the teachings of the Bible undermines the transformative power of Scripture in individuals' lives and communities. By striving to understand, internalize, and practice its teachings authentically, individuals can cultivate a genuine, impactful faith that reflects the love, compassion, humility, and justice exemplified by Jesus Christ.

Encouraging Superficial Faith

Encouraging superficial faith through the mere quoting of the Bible without understanding perpetuates a culture where individuals rely on surface-level engagement rather than fostering a deep, personal relationship with Christian teachings. Here's a closer look at this issue:

Rote Memorization Over Understanding

Quoting the Bible without understanding may encourage rote memorization of verses rather than genuine comprehension.

Individuals may recite passages without truly grasping their significance or relevance, leading to a superficial understanding of Scripture.

Lack of Personal Connection

Superficial quoting of the Bible can result in a lack of personal connection to its teachings.

Without understanding, individuals may struggle to relate biblical principles to their experiences, beliefs, and struggles, hindering the development of a meaningful faith.

Fragile Faith

Superficial engagement with Scripture can contribute to a fragile faith that lacks depth and resilience.

When individuals' faith is based solely on memorized verses or outward displays of religious devotion, it may crumble in the face of doubts, challenges, or adversity.

Shallow Application

Without understanding, individuals may apply biblical teachings shallowly or superficially.

Rather than wrestling with the complexities of Scripture and its implications for their lives, they may resort to simplistic or legalistic interpretations that fail to address more profound questions of faith and morality.

Missed Opportunities for Growth

Superficial engagement with Scripture represents a missed opportunity for spiritual growth and maturity.

Without understanding, individuals may miss out on the transformative power of the Bible to challenge, inspire, and shape their character and values.

Cultivating Depth in Faith

Cultivating depth in faith requires a commitment to understanding, internalizing, and applying the teachings of the Bible.

This involves engaging with Scripture through prayerful reflection, study, and dialogue with others, allowing its truths to penetrate the heart and mind and transform one's life.

In summary, encouraging superficial faith through merely quoting the Bible without understanding undermines the depth and resilience of individuals' spiritual lives. Christian communities can nurture a vibrant, authentic faith capable of withstanding life's challenges by fostering a culture of genuine engagement with Scripture—rooted in awareness, personal connection, and application.

Promoting Division

Promoting division within religious communities - often stems from misinterpreting and misusing biblical texts. Here's a closer examination of this issue:

Misinterpretation Leading to Disagreement

Misinterpreting biblical texts can lead to divergent understandings and interpretations among individuals or groups within a religious community.

Different interpretations of the same verses may result in disagreements and conflicts, especially when people lack a comprehensive understanding of the broader biblical narrative and principles.

Selective Use of Scripture

Individuals or factions may selectively use biblical texts to support their beliefs or agendas while ignoring or dismissing alternative interpretations.

This selective use of Scripture can create divisions within religious communities as conflicting interpretations of critical passages emerge.

Absence of Contextual Understanding

Individuals may misinterpret their meaning or significance without understanding biblical texts' historical, cultural, and literary context.

Differences in interpretation often arise when people fail to consider the context in which biblical passages were written, leading to conflicting views on their application to contemporary issues.

Lack of Dialogue and Understanding

Division within religious communities can be exacerbated by a lack of open dialogue and mutual understanding among members.

When individuals or groups hold rigid interpretations of Scripture without the willingness to engage in respectful dialogue or consider alternative viewpoints, conflicts may escalate, and divisions may deepen.

Impact on Community Cohesion

Division fueled by misinterpretation of biblical texts can erode community cohesion and undermine the unity of religious groups.

Fractures within a community can weaken collective efforts towards shared goals, hinder mutual support and collaboration, and diminish the effectiveness of the community's witness and mission.

Promoting Unity Through Education and Dialogue

Promoting unity within religious communities requires education, dialogue, and a commitment to understanding and respecting diverse perspectives.

Communities can work towards reconciliation and unity by fostering an environment where members can engage in open and respectful discussion, deepen their understanding of Scripture, and seek common ground based on shared values and principles.

In summary, misinterpreting and misusing biblical texts can promote division within religious communities. By fostering a culture of dialogue, education, and mutual respect for diverse interpretations, communities can mitigate conflicts, encourage unity, and work towards a shared understanding of Scripture that honors its message of love, compassion, and reconciliation.

Steps To Avoid These Pitfalls

A comprehensive study of the Bible involves engaging in regular, systematic exploration of its teachings, themes, and historical context. Here's a closer look at the importance of comprehensive study and some strategies for deepening your understanding:

Understanding Context

Context is crucial for interpreting biblical passages accurately. Study the Bible's historical, cultural, and literary context to grasp its teachings' meaning.

Explore the biblical world's social, political, and religious background to gain insights into the significance of various passages.

Exploring Themes and Motifs

Identify recurring themes, motifs, and narratives throughout the Bible. Study how these themes develop and intersect across different books and genres.

Trace the overarching narrative of salvation history, from creation to redemption, to understand the unity and coherence of Scripture.

Using Study Guides and Commentaries

Utilize study guides, commentaries, and other resources to deepen your understanding of the Bible.

Consult reputable sources that provide insights into biblical texts' historical, cultural, and theological aspects.

Engaging with Different Perspectives

Explore diverse interpretations and perspectives on biblical passages. Consider how different theological traditions and scholars approach the text.

Engage in respectful dialogue with others who may have differing interpretations, recognizing the richness of diverse perspectives.

Applying Biblical Principles

Reflect on how the teachings of the Bible apply to your life and circumstances. Consider how you can live out biblical principles in your relationships, work, and community.

Seek guidance from the Holy Spirit in discerning the practical implications of Scripture for your daily life.

Cultivating a Lifelong Habit

A comprehensive study of the Bible is a lifelong journey. Cultivate a habit of regular study and reflection, making time for Scripture reading, prayer, and meditation.

Approach the Bible with humility and openness, recognizing there is always more to learn and discover about God's word.

In summary, a comprehensive study of the Bible is essential for deepening your understanding of its message and applying its teachings to your life. By engaging in systematic research, exploring diverse perspectives, and seeking guidance from reputable resources, you can enrich your spiritual journey and grow in wisdom and faith.

Seek Guidance

Seeking guidance from knowledgeable teachers, scholars, and religious leaders is invaluable for gaining deeper insights into biblical passages' historical, cultural, and theological contexts. Here's a closer look at the importance of seeking guidance and how it can enrich your understanding of the Bible:

Accessing Expertise

Knowledgeable teachers, scholars, and religious leaders possess expertise in biblical studies, theology, and related fields.

They can offer nuanced interpretations and insights that may not be readily apparent to the average reader, enriching your understanding of Scripture.

Exploring Historical and Cultural Contexts

Teachers and scholars can provide valuable context for understanding the historical and cultural background of biblical passages.

By learning about the ancient Near East's social, political, and religious dynamics, you can better appreciate the meaning and significance of biblical narratives and teachings.

Navigating Complex Theological Issues

Religious leaders and theologians can help you navigate complex theological issues the Bible raises.

They can guide interpreting challenging passages, reconciling apparent contradictions, and understanding the broader theological themes woven throughout Scripture.

Interpreting Scripture in Community

Engaging with knowledgeable teachers serd religious leaders allows you to interpret Scripture in the community.

By participating in discussions, asking questions, and exchanging ideas with others, you can gain fresh perspectives and deepen your understanding of biblical texts.

Receiving Personalized Guidance

Seek guidance tailored to your specific questions, interests, and spiritual needs.

Religious leaders and mentors can provide personalized support and direction, helping you apply biblical principles to your unique life circumstances.

Discerning Truth and Wisdom

Ultimately, seeking guidance from knowledgeable sources helps you discern truth and wisdom from the vast richness of the biblical text.

You can grow in wisdom, faith, and understanding by learning from those who study and teach Scripture.

In summary, seeking guidance from knowledgeable teachers, scholars, and religious leaders is essential for deepening your understanding of the Bible. By tapping into their expertise, you can gain valuable insights into the historical, cultural, and theological dimensions of Scripture, enriching your spiritual journey and fostering a deeper relationship with God.

Contextual Reading

Contextual reading of the Bible is crucial for understanding the intended meaning of a verse within its broader framework. Here's a deeper exploration of the importance of contextual reading and how it enhances comprehension:

Understanding Historical and Cultural Context

Contextual reading involves considering the historical and cultural background of a biblical passage.

By understanding the social, political, and religious context in which a passage was written, readers can grasp its intended meaning more accurately.

Appreciating Literary Context

Each verse is part of a larger literary context within its chapter, book, and biblical narrative.

Contextual reading requires examining the surrounding verses, chapters, and books to discern the flow of thought and thematic connections.

Avoiding Misinterpretation

Quoting a verse out of context can lead to misinterpretation and misunderstanding.

By considering the verses before and after, as well as the overall message of the book and the Bible, readers can avoid misconstruing the meaning of a passage.

Recognizing Authorial Intent

Understanding the context helps readers discern the author's original intent behind a passage.

By placing themselves in the shoes of the original audience and considering the author's cultural and historical context, readers can better appreciate the intended message.

Grasping Thematic Significance

Contextual reading allows readers to grasp the thematic significance of a passage within the broader narrative of Scripture.

Readers can discern God's word's overarching message and purpose by tracing recurring themes, motifs, and narratives throughout the Bible.

Promoting Deeper Reflection

Contextual reading prompts readers to engage in deeper reflection and study of Scripture.

By delving into the context of a passage, readers can uncover layers of meaning and application that may not be immediately apparent, leading to a richer understanding of God's truth.

In summary, a contextual reading of the Bible is essential for unlocking its profound meaning and relevance. By considering a passage's historical, cultural, and literary context, readers can discern its intended message, avoid misinterpretation, and engage more deeply with the transformative power of God's word.

Reflect And Meditate

Reflecting on and meditating on Scripture is fundamental for deepening spiritual understanding and personal growth. Here's a closer look at the importance of reflection and meditation, along with some strategies for incorporating them into your spiritual life:

Engaging with Scripture

Reflection and meditation allow you to engage with Scripture beyond surface-level reading.

Rather than simply skimming through verses, take the time to ponder their meaning, relevance, and implications for your life.

Asking Questions

Use reflection as an opportunity to ask questions about the text. Consider the passage's who, what, when, where, why, and how.

Asking questions can deepen your understanding and lead to insights that may not be immediately apparent.

Seeking Deeper Meanings

Reflective meditation encourages you to seek deeper meanings and insights within Scripture.

Look beyond the literal interpretation of the text and explore its symbolic, metaphorical, and spiritual significance.

Praying for Understanding and Wisdom

Prayer is an essential component of reflection and meditation on Scripture.

Pray for understanding, wisdom, and guidance as you engage with God's word, inviting the Holy Spirit to illuminate its meaning and relevance.

Creating Sacred Space

Create a sacred space for reflection and meditation, free from distractions and interruptions.

Find a quiet place to immerse yourself in Scripture and connect with God in prayer and contemplation.

Journaling and Contemplation

Consider journaling to document your reflections, insights, and prayers.

Journaling can help you track your spiritual journey, process your thoughts and emotions, and discern God's leading.

Incorporating Reflection into Daily Life

Make reflection and meditation on Scripture a regular part of your daily routine.

Set aside dedicated time each day for prayerful reflection, meditation, and study of God's word, allowing it to shape your thoughts, attitudes, and actions.

In summary, reflecting on and meditating on Scripture is a transformative practice that deepens your understanding of God's word and fosters spiritual growth. You can cultivate a more prosperous, meaningful relationship with God and His word by asking questions, seeking deeper meanings, praying for understanding, and creating a sacred space for contemplation.

Practice Application

Practicing the application of biblical principles in everyday life is essential for truly understanding and embodying the teachings of the Bible. Here's a deeper exploration of the importance of application and how to integrate biblical principles into daily living:

Living Out Faith

Applying biblical principles involves putting faith into action through daily choices, attitudes, and behaviors.

Rather than treat the Bible as theoretical or abstract, strive to live out its teachings practically.

Integrating Faith and Life

Integrate biblical principles into all areas of life, including relationships, work, finances, and decision-making.

Seek to align your thoughts, words, and actions with the values and teachings of Scripture, allowing faith to permeate every aspect of your life.

Modeling Christ-Like Behavior

Application of biblical principles entails modeling Christ-like behavior in your interactions with others.

Practice love, compassion, forgiveness, humility, and service in your relationships and daily encounters, reflecting the character of Christ to those around you.

Seeking Guidance from Scripture

Turn to the Bible as guidance and wisdom for navigating life's challenges and decisions.

Let biblical principles shape your attitudes, priorities, and responses to various situations, providing a solid foundation for ethical and moral decision-making.

Continual Growth and Transformation

Application of biblical principles is a journey of continual growth and transformation.

Be open to the Holy Spirit's leading and conviction, allowing God's word to challenge, convict, and shape you into whom He desires you to be.

Accountability and Support

Seek accountability and support from fellow believers in living out biblical principles.

Surround yourself with a community of faith that encourages, challenges, and holds you accountable in your walk with God.

Reflecting God's Love and Grace

Applying biblical principles reflects God's love, grace, and truth.

Through your words and actions, be a living testimony to the transformative power of God's word, inviting others to experience the life-changing impact of faith in Christ.

In summary, practicing applying biblical principles in everyday life is a vital aspect of understanding and embodying the teachings of the Bible. By integrating faith into all areas of life, modeling Christ-like behavior, seeking guidance from Scripture, and fostering continual growth and transformation, you can live out the transformative power of God's word and be a light in the world.

Encourage Dialogue

Encouraging dialogue about biblical teachings is an enriching practice that can lead to new insights and a deeper understanding of Scripture. Here's a closer look at the importance of dialogue and how it enhances our knowledge of the Bible:

Exchanging Perspectives

Dialogue allows for the exchange of diverse perspectives on biblical teachings.

Engaging with others with different interpretations or experiences can broaden your understanding and challenge preconceived notions.

Stimulating Critical Thinking

Discussing biblical teachings stimulates critical thinking and intellectual engagement.

Participants can deepen their understanding and refine their beliefs by questioning, analyzing, and evaluating different viewpoints.

Fostering Learning and Growth

Dialogue fosters a learning environment where individuals can grow in their knowledge and understanding of Scripture.

By listening to others' insights and sharing them, participants can glean new understandings and perspectives that contribute to their spiritual growth.

Building Community

Dialogue fosters a sense of community and connection among believers.

Participants build relationships based on mutual respect, understanding, and shared faith by coming together to discuss and explore biblical teachings.

Respecting Diversity

Dialogue promotes respect for diversity within the body of Christ.

Recognizing that different individuals may interpret Scripture differently allows for a spirit of humility, openness, and acceptance within the community.

Seeking Truth Together

Dialogue is a collaborative process of seeking truth together.

By engaging in respectful and constructive conversations, participants can work towards a deeper understanding of God's word and its application to their lives.

Practicing Humility and Openness

Dialogue cultivates humility and openness to new ideas and perspectives.

Participants approach discussions with a willingness to listen, learn, and grow, recognizing that no one has a monopoly on truth and everyone has something valuable to contribute.

In summary, encouraging dialogue about biblical teachings is a valuable practice that promotes learning, growth, and community within the body of Christ. By exchanging perspectives, stimulating critical thinking, fostering learning and development, building community, respecting diversity, seeking truth together, and practicing humility and openness, participants can deepen their understanding of Scripture and enrich their spiritual journey together. By striving for a genuine sense of the Bible, individuals can quote and apply its teachings more accurately and meaningfully, fostering a deeper and more authentic faith.

Love And Acceptance Vs. Hate And Discrimination

Core Tenets Of Christianity: Love And Acceptance

At the heart of Christianity lie two core tenets: love and acceptance. These foundational principles permeate the teachings of Jesus Christ and serve as the guiding ethos for believers worldwide.

Love

Love for God: Christianity teaches that love is the highest commandment, with Jesus declaring that loving God with all one's heart, soul, and mind is the greatest commandment.

Love for Others: The command to love one's neighbor as oneself is central to Christian doctrine. This inclusive love extends to all individuals, regardless of race, ethnicity, social status, or belief system.

Agape Love: Christian love, often referred to as agape love, is characterized by selflessness, compassion, and sacrificial action. It embodies putting others' needs before oneself, seeking well-being, and flourishing.

Acceptance

Acceptance of Diversity: Christianity emphasizes accepting diversity and recognizing the inherent worth and dignity of every individual as a creation of God. This acceptance extends to people of all backgrounds, cultures, and identities.

Forgiveness and Redemption: The concept of forgiveness and redemption is central to Christian theology. Christians are called to extend grace and forgiveness to others, recognizing that all individuals are fallible and need redemption.

Inclusivity and Welcome: Christianity advocates for inclusivity and welcomes all individuals into the community of believers, regardless of their past mistakes or current circumstances. It rejects exclusionary practices and embraces a message of hospitality and openness.

Integration of Love and Acceptance

Love as the Foundation: Love is the foundation upon which acceptance is built. Genuine acceptance stems from a place of love and compassion, reflecting Christ's unconditional love for all humanity.

Practical Expression: Love and acceptance are not merely abstract concepts, but practical expression is found in acts of kindness, compassion, and service towards others. Christians are called to embody these values in their daily interactions and relationships.

Radical Inclusivity: Christianity espouses a vision of radical inclusivity, where love and acceptance transcend societal boundaries and embrace individuals from all walks of life. This inclusive vision challenges cultural norms and prejudices, fostering a community characterized by unity, diversity, and mutual respect.

Challenges and Growth

Overcoming Prejudice: Despite Christianity's emphasis on love and acceptance, adherents may still struggle with prejudices and biases. Overcoming these challenges requires introspection, humility, and a commitment to learning and growth.

Extending Grace: Practicing love and acceptance - often involves extending grace to those with different beliefs or lifestyles. It requires a willingness to engage in dialogue, empathize with others' experiences, and seek common ground amidst differences.

Social Justice: Love and acceptance compel Christians to advocate for social justice and equality, challenging oppression and discrimination and undermining marginalized communities' dignity and rights.

In summary, love and acceptance are core tenets of Christianity that underpin its ethical framework and shape believers' attitudes and actions toward others. Embracing these values fosters a community characterized by compassion, inclusivity, and hospitality, reflecting the transformative power of Christ's love in the world. As Christians strive to embody these principles, they contribute to building a more just, equitable, and compassionate society for all.

Contrast With Manifestations Of Hate And

Discrimination Within Christian Communities

Contrast with manifestations of hate and discrimination within Christian communities highlights the stark divergence between the core teachings of Christianity, centered on love and acceptance, and the unfortunate reality of prejudice and exclusion that can occur within religious contexts. This concept explores the tension between Christian ideals and the manifestations of hate and discrimination, examining their underlying causes, consequences, and potential avenues for reconciliation and transformation.

Roots of Hate and Discrimination

Misinterpretation of Scripture: Hate and discrimination within Christian communities can stem from misinterpretations or selective readings of religious texts, where specific passages are used to justify discriminatory attitudes or exclusionary practices.

Cultural Influences: Sociocultural factors such as nationalism, ethnocentrism, or historical prejudices may infiltrate Christian communities, distorting their perception of others and fostering discriminatory attitudes based on race, ethnicity, gender, sexuality, or religious affiliation.

Fear and Insecurity: Hate and discrimination often arise from fear and insecurity, as individuals perceive those who are different as threats to their identity, values, or way of life, leading to scapegoating, stereotyping, or marginalization.

Lack of Empathy: A lack of empathy or understanding toward others' experiences and struggles can contribute to the dehumanization and vilification of specific groups within Christian communities, perpetuating cycles of hate and discrimination.

Manifestations of Hate and Discrimination

Racial Prejudice: Racism and racial prejudice persist within some Christian communities, manifesting in attitudes of superiority, segregation, or exclusion towards people of different racial or ethnic backgrounds.

Homophobia and Transphobia: LGBTQ+ individuals often face discrimination within Christian communities, where their identities and relationships may be condemned as sinful or deviant, leading to exclusion, harassment, or violence.

Gender Discrimination: Some Christian traditions uphold patriarchal norms and gender roles that limit the roles and opportunities available to women, reinforcing attitudes of inequality and discrimination within religious institutions.

Religious Intolerance: Religious intolerance can occur within Christian communities towards adherents of other faiths or denominations, leading to hostility, proselytization, or efforts to suppress religious freedom and diversity.

Social Exclusion: Certain groups, such as the poor, homeless, or marginalized, may experience social exclusion or neglect within Christian communities, where their needs and voices are overlooked or dismissed.

Consequences of Hate and Discrimination

Spiritual Harm: Hate and discrimination undermine the spiritual integrity and witness of Christian communities, alienating individuals and distorting the message of love and acceptance at the heart of Christianity.

Interpersonal Conflict: Discriminatory attitudes can lead to interpersonal conflict and division within Christian communities, eroding trust, unity, and mutual respect among believers.

Loss of Credibility: Christian communities that perpetuate hate and discrimination risk losing credibility and relevance in the eyes of society, tarnishing their reputation as agents of love, justice, and reconciliation.

Psychological Harm: Hate and discrimination inflict psychological harm on individuals who are targeted, leading to feelings of shame, rejection, or self-doubt and undermining their sense of worth and belonging within the faith community.

Addressing Hate and Discrimination

Educational Initiatives: Education and awareness-raising efforts within Christian communities can challenge stereotypes, debunk myths, and promote understanding and empathy towards marginalized groups.

Promotion of Diversity: Promoting diversity and inclusion within Christian communities celebrates the richness of God's creation and affirms the dignity and worth of all individuals, regardless of their backgrounds or identities.

Advocacy for Social Justice: Christians are called to advocate for social justice and equality, challenging systems of oppression and discrimination that undermine the dignity and rights of marginalized communities.

Reconciliation and Healing: Christian communities can foster reconciliation and healing by acknowledging past injustices, seeking forgiveness, and working towards restoration and restitution with those harmed by hate and discrimination.

In summary, the contrast with manifestations of hate and discrimination within Christian communities underscores the urgent need for self-reflection, accountability, and transformation within the Church. By confronting the roots and consequences of hate and prejudice, Christians can strive towards a more faithful embodiment of the teachings of Jesus Christ, marked by love, compassion, and radical inclusion for all.

Exploration Of The Disconnect Between Doctrine And Practice

Exploration of the disconnect between doctrine and practice delves into the paradoxical phenomenon where a religious tradition's professed beliefs and teachings diverge from its adherents' actual behaviors and actions. This concept examines the underlying factors contributing to this disconnect, its implications for religious communities, and potential strategies for reconciliation and alignment between doctrine and practice.

Roots of the Disconnect

Human Fallibility: The disconnect often arises from the inherent fallibility of human beings, who may struggle to fully embody or enact the ideals and values espoused by their religious tradition due to personal weaknesses, temptations, or limitations.

Cultural Context: Sociocultural factors, including societal norms, values, and pressures, can influence individuals' behaviors and practices, leading to discrepancies between religious doctrine and societal expectations.

Historical Context: Historical factors, such as political upheavals, cultural shifts, or religious schisms, may shape the development and interpretation of spiritual teachings, resulting in divergent understandings and applications of doctrine.

Individual Interpretation: The subjective interpretation of religious teachings and scriptures can vary among believers, leading to differences in understanding and application of doctrine, which may contribute to inconsistencies in practice.

Manifestations of the Disconnect

Hypocrisy: The most glaring manifestation of the disconnect is hypocrisy, where individuals profess adherence to religious principles while engaging in behaviors or actions that contradict those principles, leading to a perceived lack of authenticity or integrity.

Selective Application: Believers may selectively apply religious teachings, adhering to certain aspects of doctrine while ignoring or rationalizing away others, resulting in inconsistencies in behavior or moral decision-making.

Cultural Adaptation: Religious practices may be adapted or modified to fit within cultural norms or societal expectations, sometimes at the expense of fidelity to doctrinal teachings, leading to syncretism or compromise.

Institutional Corruption: Institutional structures within religious organizations may become corrupted, prioritizing power, control, or self-interest over the ethical principles and values of the faith tradition, resulting in systemic injustices or abuses.

Implications and Challenges

Erosion of Credibility: The disconnect between doctrine and practice can undermine the credibility and moral authority of religious institutions, leading to disillusionment, skepticism, or disengagement among believers and society at large.

Loss of Moral Compass: When religious teachings are not reflected in practice, believers may lack a moral compass or ethical framework for navigating life's challenges, contributing to moral ambiguity or moral relativism.

Interpersonal Conflict: Inconsistencies between doctrine and practice may lead to interpersonal conflict or division within religious communities as individuals grapple with differing interpretations or expectations of religious behavior.

Missed Opportunities for Growth: The disconnect between doctrine and practice represents a missed opportunity for personal and communal growth, as believers may fail to fully embody the transformative potential of their faith tradition in their lives and relationships.

Strategies for Reconciliation

Introspection and Self-Reflection: Believers can engage in introspection and self-reflection to identify areas of discrepancy between their professed beliefs and actual behaviors, seeking alignment and integrity in their spiritual journey.

Education and Discipleship: Religious education and discipleship programs can deepen believers' understanding of doctrine and its practical implications, empowering them to live out their faith with greater authenticity and consistency.

Accountability and Community Support: Establishing accountability structures and fostering supportive communities can help believers uphold their commitments to religious principles and hold one another accountable for their actions and behaviors.

Social Justice and Advocacy: Active engagement in social justice and advocacy initiatives aligns religious principles with concrete actions, translating doctrine into tangible efforts to promote justice, equality, and compassion in society.

Exploring the disconnect between doctrine and practice reveals the complex interplay of individual, cultural, and institutional factors shaping religious identity and behavior. By acknowledging and addressing this disconnect with humility, honesty, and a commitment to transformative action, believers can work towards a more authentic and integrated expression of their faith, fostering greater coherence between their professed beliefs and lived experiences.

Do You Hate Because That's How You Feel Or Because

Someone Taught You To Hate?

Asking oneself whether they hate because it aligns with their true feelings or because they have been taught to hate is an essential inquiry into the roots of one's emotions and attitudes. This reflective question prompts individuals to examine the origins of their hatred or hostility towards others, whether they stem from personal experiences, societal influences, or learned behaviors.

Here are some points to consider when exploring this question:

Reflecting on Personal Emotions: Take time to reflect on your emotions and feelings towards others. Are your feelings of hate or animosity genuine expressions of your inner state, or are they influenced by external factors or conditioning?

Examining Learned Behaviors: Consider whether your attitudes and beliefs about certain groups or individuals have been shaped by external influences, such as family, peers, media, or societal norms. Have you adopted hateful attitudes as a result of exposure to prejudiced or discriminatory messages?

Assessing Personal Experiences: Reflect on your personal experiences and interactions with individuals or groups that you harbor feelings of hate towards. Have negative experiences or conflicts fueled your feelings of hostility, or are they based on generalized stereotypes or prejudices?

Exploring Cultural and Social Influences: Consider the role of cultural and social factors in shaping attitudes towards certain groups or individuals. Have you been influenced by societal narratives or cultural norms that promote division, prejudice, or intolerance?

Analyzing Group Dynamics: Evaluate the influence of group dynamics on your feelings of hate or animosity. Have you adopted hateful attitudes to conform to group norms or gain acceptance within a particular social circle?

Questioning Belief Systems: Challenge the belief systems or ideologies that may underlie feelings of hate or animosity. Are your attitudes based on legitimate grievances or injustices rooted in unfounded stereotypes, biases, or misinformation?

Considering Empathy and Understanding: Cultivate empathy and understanding towards those you harbor feelings of hate towards. Try to put yourself in their shoes and consider the factors contributing to their actions or behaviors. Are there underlying fears, insecurities, or traumas that drive their behavior?

Practicing Self-Reflection: Engage in regular self-reflection to examine the sources of your feelings of hate or animosity. Are there unresolved conflicts, traumas, or insecurities within yourself that may be contributing to these negative emotions?

Seeking Healing and Growth: Explore avenues for healing and growth that can help you address and overcome feelings of hate or animosity. Are there practices such as therapy, mindfulness, or forgiveness that can help you cultivate a more compassionate and empathetic outlook?

Reflecting on Personal Values: Consider how your values align with feelings of hate or animosity. Do these emotions conflict with your core values of empathy, compassion, and respect for others, or do they reflect a departure from your values?

Analyzing Media Consumption: Reflect on the media sources you consume and their potential impact on your attitudes and beliefs. Have you been exposed to content that promotes hate or division, and how has this influenced your perceptions of others?

Examining Peer Influence: Evaluate the influence of peers and social circles on your feelings of hate or animosity. Are you surrounded by individuals who reinforce negative attitudes towards certain groups or individuals, and how does this affect your beliefs?

Considering Power Dynamics: Reflect on the role of power dynamics in shaping attitudes of hate or discrimination. Are your feelings of hate directed toward marginalized or oppressed groups? And if so, how do issues of privilege and power contribute to these emotions?

Exploring Historical Context: Consider the historical context in which attitudes of hate and discrimination have been perpetuated. Have historical events or societal structures contributed to the normalization of hate, and how does this impact present-day attitudes?

Questioning Fear-Based Motivations: Explore whether feelings of hate or hatred are rooted in fear. Are you motivated by a fear of the unknown, a fear of losing power or privilege, or a fear of difference, and how does this impact your perceptions of others?

Practicing Empathy and Perspective-Taking: Cultivate empathy by understanding the experiences and perspectives of those you harbor feelings of hate towards. Are there underlying factors such as trauma, discrimination, or systemic injustice that contribute to their behavior?

Engaging in Dialogue: Foster open dialogue and communication with individuals or groups you feel hatred towards. Are there opportunities to engage in constructive conversations that promote understanding and reconciliation, and how can you approach these interactions with an open mind?

Committing to Anti-Hate Advocacy: Take proactive steps to combat hate and discrimination in your community and society. Are there organizations or initiatives that you can support or get involved with promoting tolerance, inclusion, and social justice?

Reflecting on Personal Responsibility: Consider your responsibility to perpetuate or challenge feelings of hate. Are you actively contributing to a culture of intolerance through your words, actions, or silence, or are you taking steps to promote empathy and understanding?

Exploring Intersectionality: Reflect on how intersecting aspects of identity, such as race, gender, sexuality, and socio-economic status, influence experiences of hate and discrimination. Are you mindful of the multiple layers of oppression individuals may face, and how does this inform your attitudes and behaviors?

Recognizing Systemic Injustice: Acknowledge the role of systemic injustice and structural inequalities in perpetuating hate and discrimination. Are you aware of how institutionalized forms of oppression contribute to the marginalization and mistreatment of certain groups, and how can you work towards dismantling these systems?

Challenging Implicit Bias: Examine your implicit biases and unconscious prejudices that may contribute to feelings of hate or animosity. Are you willing to confront and challenge these biases through education, self-reflection, and anti-racism work?

Promoting Diversity and Inclusion: Commit to promoting diversity, equity, and inclusion in all aspects of your life. Are you actively seeking diverse perspectives and experiences, advocating for inclusive policies and practices, and creating spaces welcoming and celebrating differences?

Empowering Marginalized Voices: Amplify the voices and experiences of marginalized individuals and communities most impacted by hate and discrimination. Are you listening to and centering the narratives of those directly affected and using your privilege to advocate for their rights and dignity?

Cultivating Compassion and Forgiveness: Practice compassion and forgiveness towards yourself and others as you navigate feelings of hate or animosity. Can you extend grace and understanding, even in challenging circumstances, and work towards healing and reconciliation?

Educating Yourself: Take proactive steps to educate yourself about the historical and contemporary manifestations of hate and discrimination. Are you seeking resources, literature, and learning opportunities that deepen your understanding of these issues and empower you to take meaningful action?

Building Community and Solidarity: Foster connections and solidarity with individuals and groups committed to combating hate and promoting social justice. Are you actively participating in collective efforts to address systemic oppression, build alliances, and create positive change?

Celebrating Love and Humanity: Embrace love, empathy, and humanity as guiding principles in your interactions with others. Are you committed to fostering a culture of love and acceptance that celebrates every individual's inherent worth and dignity, regardless of differences?

By reflecting on these points, individuals can further explore the complexities of hate and discrimination and identify concrete actions to contribute to a more just, equitable, and compassionate world. This ongoing process of self-examination and activism is essential in creating lasting social change and promoting the well-being of all members of society.

Choosing Religion Over Family And Health

Understanding The Conflict

Religious devotion often demands significant time, energy, and resources, creating tension when these obligations precede family responsibilities or personal well-being. This conflict can manifest in several ways:

Neglecting Family Time for Religious Activities

Devout individuals may spend extensive hours attending religious services, participating in community events, or engaging in personal worship. While these activities are spiritually fulfilling, they can limit the time available for family interactions and shared experiences. This can lead to neglect or resentment among family members who may feel sidelined by religious commitments.

Adhering to Religious Practices That May Impact Health

Some religious practices involve fasting, dietary restrictions, or physical exertions that can affect one's health. For instance, prolonged fasting might lead to nutritional deficiencies or other health issues. At the same time, strict dietary laws might restrict access to certain nutrients. When religious adherence negatively impacts health, it creates a dilemma between maintaining spiritual integrity and ensuring personal well-being.

Placing Religious Beliefs Above Familial Relationships

Conflicts can arise when religious beliefs clash with family values or practices. For example, interfaith marriages, differing religious practices within the same household, or disagreements about raising children in a particular faith can strain familial bonds. Sometimes, individuals may prioritize their religious beliefs over family relationships, leading to alienation or division within the family.

Economic and Resource Allocation

Financial contributions to religious institutions or funding religious activities can sometimes strain a family's budget. The allocation of resources towards religious causes might be perceived as a burden, significantly if it impacts the family's ability to meet essential needs or pursue personal goals. This economic strain can lead to conflicts about financial priorities and responsibilities.

Emotional and Psychological Strain

Balancing religious devotion with family responsibilities can be emotionally taxing. The pressure to fulfill both religious and familial roles can lead to stress, guilt, or burnout. Individuals might feel torn between their duty to their faith and their commitment to their family, causing internal conflict and emotional distress.

Social and Cultural Expectations

Societal and cultural expectations regarding religious observance can exacerbate conflicts. In some communities, there may be intense pressure to conform to religious norms, which can intensify the struggle to balance these demands with personal and familial needs. This external pressure can amplify feelings of inadequacy or failure when individuals cannot meet all expectations.

Navigating these conflicts requires open communication, mutual understanding, and a willingness to find compromises that honor religious devotion and family commitments. Families can benefit from discussing their needs and boundaries, seeking common ground, and supporting each other in maintaining a healthy balance between spiritual practices and personal well-being.

Biblical Perspective

The Bible provides nuanced guidance on balancing religious devotion with family responsibilities and personal well-being. These teachings sometimes appear conflicting, but they aim to foster a holistic approach to living a faithful and balanced life.

Loving God Above All Else

In Matthew 10:37-39, Jesus emphasizes the primacy of devotion to God:

Matthew 10:37-39: "Anyone who loves their father or mother more than me is not worthy of me; anyone who loves their son or daughter more than me is not worthy of me. Whoever does not take up their cross and follow me is not worthy of me. Whoever finds their life will lose it, and whoever loses their life for my sake will find it."

Interpretation: This passage underscores the necessity of placing one's relationship with God above all earthly attachments, including family. It speaks to the ultimate commitment required of a follower of Christ, where the love for God must surpass all other loves.

The Importance of Family

However, the Bible also provides clear instructions on the significance of familial responsibilities and relationships:

Ephesians 5:25-29: "Husbands, love your wives, just as Christ loved the church and gave himself up for her to make her holy, cleansing her by the washing with water through the word, and to present her to himself as a radiant church, without stain or wrinkle or any other blemish, but holy and blameless. In this same way, husbands should love their wives as their bodies. He who loves his wife loves himself."

Interpretation: This passage highlights the deep commitment and love that should exist within a marriage, comparing it to Christ's love for the church. It emphasizes selfless love, care, and the responsibility to nurture and protect one's spouse.

Ephesians 6:1-4: "Children, obey your parents in the Lord, for this is right. 'Honor your father and mother'—the first commandment with a promise—' so that it may go well with you and you may enjoy long life on the earth.' Fathers, do not exasperate your children; instead, bring them up in the training and instruction of the Lord."

Interpretation: This passage stresses the importance of familial relationships, especially the duties of children to their parents and parents to their children. It calls for mutual respect, proper upbringing, and nurturing within the family.

The Importance of Health

The Bible also recognizes the importance of physical health and well-being:

1 Corinthians 6:19-20: "Do you not know that your bodies are temples of the Holy Spirit, who is in you, whom you have received from God? You are not your; you were bought at a price. Therefore, honor God with your bodies."

Interpretation: This passage frames the body as a sacred vessel that houses the Holy Spirit. It emphasizes the responsibility to maintain and honor one's physical health as an act of worship and reverence to God.

Reconciling These Perspectives

Balancing these biblical principles requires a holistic and integrated approach:

Prioritize Spiritual Devotion: Recognize the importance of placing God at the center of one's life. This primary devotion should inspire and guide all other aspects of living, including relationships and personal care.

Honor Family Commitments: Understand that genuine devotion to God naturally extends to loving and caring for one's family. Love and responsibility towards family are not separate from religious duties; they express one's faith.

Maintain Physical Health: Viewing the body as a temple encourages believers to care for their physical health. This care is part of a broader spiritual discipline that respects the sanctity of life and health.

Seek Balance and Wisdom: Apply wisdom in balancing these responsibilities. This might involve setting healthy boundaries, ensuring quality family time, and maintaining one's health to serve God and family effectively.

In summary, the Bible calls for a balanced life where devotion to God enhances rather than diminishes the love for family and care for oneself. By integrating these principles, individuals can strive to live a faithful, healthy, and harmonious life.

Balancing Faith, Family, And Health

Maintaining a balance between religious devotion, family responsibilities, and personal health is crucial for a harmonious and fulfilling life. Here are vital considerations to help achieve this balance:

Faith and Family

Integration

Family Prayers and Worship: Engage in family prayers, attend religious services together, and participate in faith-based activities as a unit. This not only strengthens the family bond but also nurtures spiritual growth collectively.

Shared Values and Practices: Incorporate religious values into daily family routines. For example, sharing meals with blessings, discussing moral lessons from religious texts, and celebrating religious holidays together can integrate faith into family life.

Communication

Discuss Commitments: Openly discuss religious commitments and family needs. Setting clear expectations and understanding each other's priorities can help find a balance that respects both.

Schedule Coordination: Coordinate schedules to ensure that religious activities do not conflict with important family events or needs. This ensures that both aspects of life receive adequate attention.

Support

Mutual Encouragement: Encourage family members to support each other's religious and family obligations. For instance, attending each other's religious events and helping with family responsibilities can foster a supportive environment.

Shared Responsibilities: Distribute family duties in a way that allows each member to participate in their religious practices without feeling overwhelmed or neglecting family responsibilities.

Faith and Health

Self-Care

Health as Stewardship: Understand that caring for one's health is honoring God. Viewing the body as a temple, as mentioned in 1 Corinthians 6:19-20, encourages believers to prioritize their physical and mental well-being.

Rest and Nutrition: Ensure adequate rest, proper nutrition, and regular exercise. These practices are essential for maintaining the energy and health required to fulfill religious and familial duties.

Moderation

Balanced Practices: Engage in religious practices in moderation. Overextending oneself in fasting, prayer, or other spiritual disciplines can lead to physical and mental exhaustion, which is counterproductive.

Mindful Participation: Be aware of how religious activities impact health. Adjust practices to ensure they contribute positively to overall well-being rather than causing harm.

Medical Care

Faith and Medicine Coexistence: Recognize that seeking medical care is not a sign of weak faith but a responsible act of stewardship over one's health. God often works through medical professionals and treatments to bring healing.

Avoiding Extremes: Rejecting medical treatment on purely religious grounds can lead to severe health consequences. Balance faith with practical medical interventions to ensure comprehensive care.

Practical Tips for Balancing

Set Priorities

Identify Core Values: Identify the core values and priorities for faith and family. Use these values to guide decisions and actions, ensuring neither aspect is compromised.

Create a Balanced Schedule: Develop a schedule that allocates time for religious practices, family activities, and self-care. Flexibility in this schedule can help accommodate unexpected needs without stress.

Seek Guidance

Spiritual Leaders: Consult with spiritual leaders or mentors for guidance on balancing religious devotion with other life responsibilities. They can offer insights and advice based on experience and wisdom.

Health Professionals: Engage with health professionals who respect your faith and can provide advice on maintaining physical and mental health without compromising religious practices.

Foster Community

Support Networks: Build a support network within your religious community that understands and respects the balance you strive to maintain. Sharing experiences and strategies with others in similar situations can provide valuable support and encouragement.

Balancing faith, family, and health requires deliberate effort and thoughtful planning. Individuals can live a harmonious and fulfilling life that honors their spiritual and personal responsibilities by integrating faith into family life, maintaining open communication, supporting each other's commitments, and prioritizing health as stewardship.

Consequences Of Imbalance

Failing to balance religious devotion with family responsibilities and personal health can lead to severe repercussions that affect various aspects of life. Here are the critical consequences of such an imbalance:

Family Strain:

Neglect

Emotional Distance: When religious activities are prioritized over family, family members may feel neglected and unimportant. This can create emotional distance and weaken family bonds.

Resentment: Continuous neglect can lead to resentment among family members, particularly if they feel their needs and time together are consistently overlooked.

Conflict

Differing Commitments: Differences in the level of religious commitment within a family can create conflicts. For instance, one member's rigorous religious practices might clash with another member's more moderate approach, leading to disagreements and tension.

Value Clashes: If religious beliefs and practices impose strict rules that others in the family do not share, it can lead to clashes over daily routines, parenting decisions, and lifestyle choices, further straining relationships.

Health Issues:

Physical Health

Extreme Fasting: Extreme fasting or other stringent dietary restrictions can lead to nutritional deficiencies, a weakened immune system, and other health complications.

Lack of Sleep: Sacrificing sleep for extended prayer sessions or religious activities can result in chronic fatigue, decreased cognitive function, and a higher risk of various health problems, including heart disease and diabetes.

Ignoring Medical Advice: Neglecting medical advice in favor of religious rituals or beliefs can exacerbate existing health issues and prevent timely treatment of illnesses.

Mental Health

Stress and Anxiety: Excessive religious obligations can create significant stress and anxiety, particularly if individuals feel overwhelmed by the demands of their faith while trying to meet family and work responsibilities.

Burnout: Continuous overcommitment to religious activities without adequate rest and relaxation can lead to burnout, characterized by emotional exhaustion, decreased motivation, and a sense of detachment.

Guilt and Fear: Failing to meet religious expectations can lead to feelings of guilt and fear, contributing to mental health issues such as depression and anxiety.

Practical Impacts of Imbalance:

Impact on Children

Emotional Development: Children may struggle with emotional development if they feel neglected or witness constant family conflicts over religious practices.

Identity Conflicts: Children growing up in a household with conflicting religious commitments may face identity conflicts and confusion regarding their beliefs and values.

Social Consequences

Isolation: Overemphasis on religious activities can isolate individuals from broader social interactions, limiting their social support network and opportunities for personal growth.

Community Strain: Conflicts within the family over religious commitments can extend to the larger community, causing division and affecting community relationships.

Mitigating the Consequences:

Open Communication

Discuss Priorities: Regularly discuss and reassess priorities with family members to ensure everyone's needs are met and that religious practices are balanced with family time.

Set Boundaries: Establish clear boundaries to prevent religious activities from encroaching on essential family time and personal health.

Holistic Approach to Health

Integrate Self-Care: Incorporate self-care practices into religious routines, such as mindful prayer or meditation, to enhance mental well-being and reduce stress.

Seek Professional Help: Do not hesitate to seek medical and psychological help. Balancing faith with professional advice ensures comprehensive care.

Flexibility in Religious Practices:

Adapt Practices: Be flexible in religious practices to accommodate family and health needs. For example, if traditional fasting is not feasible for health reasons, consider alternative ways to observe religious duties.

By recognizing and addressing the potential consequences of imbalance, individuals can create a more harmonious and fulfilling life that respects and integrates religious devotion, family responsibilities, and personal health.

Real-Life Scenarios

Understanding how to balance religious commitment with family responsibilities and personal health can be challenging. Here are some illustrative scenarios along with possible solutions to navigate these challenges:

Scenario 1: Religious Commitment vs. Family Time

Challenge: A parent prioritizes attending church services and religious meetings over spending quality time with their children.

Illustration: Jessica is deeply involved in her church, attending multiple services, Bible study groups, and volunteer activities throughout the week. Her children feel neglected as she spends more time at church than with them.

Solution: Integrate Family into Religious Activities: Jessica can involve her children in church activities, making it a family affair. Attending services together, participating in community service as a family, and having family prayers can strengthen their bond while maintaining religious commitments.

Set Specific Family Time: Jessica should designate specific times for family bonding that do not conflict with church activities. This could include family dinners, weekend outings, or a dedicated family game night.

Prioritize Activities: Jessica can evaluate her church commitments and prioritize the essential ones, possibly reducing her involvement to ensure she has sufficient time for her family.

Scenario 2: Religious Practices and Health

Challenge: Individuals adhere to a strict fasting regimen that adversely affects their health.

Illustration: Raj follows a strict fasting regimen during religious observances. However, his rigorous work schedule and intense physical activity leave him feeling weak and dehydrated.

Solution: Modify Fasting Practices: Raj should consult religious leaders and healthcare providers to modify his fasting regimen. Adjustments could include eating nutrient-dense foods during non-fasting hours, ensuring proper hydration, and possibly altering the fasting schedule to suit his health needs.

Health Monitoring: Raj should regularly monitor his health during fasting periods and be open to making necessary adjustments if he experiences adverse effects.

Alternative Observances: If fasting severely impacts his health, Raj could explore alternative forms of observance, such as charitable acts or additional prayers, as recommended by his faith leaders.

Scenario 3: Medical Treatment vs. Faith

Challenge: Refusing medical treatment for a severe condition due to religious beliefs.

Illustration: Emily has been diagnosed with a severe illness but refuses medical treatment, believing that her faith alone will heal her. Her family is worried about her health deteriorating without proper medical intervention.

Solution: Balanced Approach: Emily can seek a balance by incorporating prayer and faith-based practices with medical treatment. She can view medical intervention as a means God provides to aid in her healing.

Religious Counseling: Emily should seek counsel from her religious leaders to discuss the importance of maintaining health while adhering to faith. Leaders can provide guidance that supports using medical treatment alongside spiritual practices.

Informed Decision-Making: Emily should educate herself on how faith and medicine coexist. Understanding that medical professionals are often seen as instruments of God's healing might alleviate her concerns and encourage her to accept necessary treatments.

Additional Considerations:

Scenario 4: Balancing Work and Religious Observance

Challenge: Balancing a demanding career with religious observances.

Illustration: John works long hours in a corporate job and finds it difficult to attend weekly religious services and participate in faith-based community activities.

Solution: Flexible Work Arrangements: John can discuss flexible working hours or remote work options with his employer to accommodate his religious observances.

Prioritizing Key Events: John can prioritize attending key religious events and find alternative ways to engage with his faith community, such as online services or evening prayer groups.

Effective Time Management: Implementing effective time management strategies can help John balance his work and religious commitments, ensuring he fulfills his professional duties without compromising his faith practices.

Scenario 5: Religious Education vs. Mainstream Education for Children

Challenge: Balancing religious education with mainstream schooling.

Illustration: Lisa and Mark want their children to receive a solid religious education without compromising their performance in mainstream academics.

Solution: Integrated Curriculum: Lisa and Mark can look for schools that integrate religious education with mainstream academics or supplement mainstream education with religious studies at home.

Balanced Schedule: They can create a balanced schedule that includes time for religious studies and academic work, ensuring their children are not overwhelmed.

Open Communication: Regularly communicate with their children about their educational needs and interests to adjust their approach, ensuring a balanced and supportive learning environment.

By exploring these scenarios and potential solutions, individuals and families can find ways to harmoniously balance their religious commitments with their family responsibilities and personal health, leading to a more fulfilling and integrated life.

Finding Harmony

Achieving harmony between faith, family, and health is a nuanced and ongoing process that requires a thoughtful and balanced approach. Here are some key strategies to help navigate this complex landscape:

Prioritize Holistically

Recognize the Interconnectedness:

Integrate Values: True religious devotion encompasses spiritual practices and the care and well-being of one's family and self. Faith, family, and health are not mutually exclusive but are interconnected components of a balanced life.

Holistic View: Adopt a holistic view where religious commitments, family responsibilities, and personal health are complementary rather than competing priorities. This perspective encourages a more integrated approach to life.

Examples: Family-Centered Faith Practices: Engage in religious activities that involve the entire family, such as family prayers, attending services together, and participating in community service as a unit. This approach strengthens family bonds while maintaining religious devotion.

Self-Care as Devotion: View self-care, including maintaining physical and mental health, as integral to religious devotion. Caring for one's body and mind can be seen in honoring the divine.

Seek Guidance

Consult Religious Leaders: Spiritual Guidance: Seek religious leaders' advice to balance religious obligations with family and health needs. They can provide insights on integrating faith with everyday life and offer flexible interpretations of religious practices when necessary.

Faith-Based Counseling: Engage in faith-based counseling or support groups that can help address conflicts between religious commitments and family or health concerns. These resources can offer practical solutions and emotional support.

Consult Healthcare Professionals:

Health and Faith: Discuss religious practices with healthcare providers to ensure they meet health needs. This is particularly important for practices like fasting, where professional advice can help modify the practice to prevent adverse health effects.

Mental Health Support: Seek professionals who respect and understand religious beliefs. They can provide strategies to manage stress, anxiety, and burnout related to spiritual and family responsibilities.

Reflect and Adjust

Regular Reflection

Assess Commitments: Regularly reflect on your faith, family, and health commitments. Assess whether you are maintaining a balance or if one area is being neglected. Reflection can help identify areas that need adjustment.

Personal Check-Ins: Conduct personal check-ins to evaluate your physical and mental well-being. Ensure your religious practices enhance your life without causing stress or health issues.

Adjust as Needed

Flexible Approach: Be willing to adjust your religious practices to fit your current life circumstances. Flexibility is critical to maintaining balance. This might involve reducing the frequency of certain activities, modifying practices, or finding new ways to incorporate faith into daily life.

Open Communication: Maintain open communication with family members about your religious commitments and their impact on family life. Encourage mutual understanding and support. Be open to feedback and ready to make changes that benefit the whole family.

Practical Strategies for Achieving Harmony

Time Management: Schedule Balance: Create a schedule that includes time for religious activities, family bonding, and self-care. Use planners or digital calendars to organize your commitments effectively.

Set Boundaries: Establish clear boundaries to protect family time and personal health. For example, designate specific times of the week for non-negotiable family activities.

Community Support: Engage in Community: Build a supportive community with similar values. This can provide additional resources, encouragement, and practical help in balancing different aspects of life.

Mutual Support Groups: Join or form support groups within your religious community where members can share experiences and offer advice on balancing faith, family, and health.

Spiritual Practices for Well-Being

Mindfulness and Meditation: Incorporate mindfulness and meditation practices that align with your faith to enhance mental well-being and reduce stress.

Physical Activity: Engage in physical activities that are spiritually fulfilling, such as yoga, which combines physical exercise with spiritual reflection.

By prioritizing holistically, seeking guidance, and regularly reflecting and adjusting, individuals can find a harmonious balance that respects their faith, nurtures their family, and maintains their health. This balanced approach leads to a more fulfilling and integrated life where all aspects are nurtured and valued.

Key Biblical References

Biblical teachings provide a framework for balancing faith, family, and health. Here are vital biblical references that emphasize these principles:

Matthew 10:37-39

Matthew 10:37-39: Prioritizing Love for God While Acknowledging the Importance of Family

Verses

Matthew 10:37-39 (NIV): "Anyone who loves their father or mother more than me is not worthy of me; anyone who loves their son or daughter more than me is not worthy of me. Whoever does not take up their cross and follow me is not worthy of me. Whoever finds their life will lose it, and whoever loses their life for my sake will find it."

Elaboration

Prioritizing Love for God: These verses emphasize the supremacy of loving God above all else, including family. This means that one's devotion to God should be the foremost priority in their life.

Balancing Family Love: While prioritizing love for God, it is essential to understand that this love should not negate the importance of family. Instead, love for God should enhance one's capacity to love and care for family members. The commitment to God calls for a holistic love that encompasses and enriches family relationships.

Application

Integrated Love: Show love for God through actions that support and nurture family bonds. For instance, family prayers and religious activities can strengthen spiritual devotion and unity.

Balanced Prioritization: Ensure that devotion to God does not come at the expense of family responsibilities. Seek ways to fulfill both spiritual and familial obligations harmoniously.

Ephesians 5:25-29; 6:1-4: Emphasizing Love and Care Within the Family

Verses:

Ephesians 5:25-29 (NIV): "Husbands, love your wives, just as Christ loved the church and gave himself up for her to make her holy, cleansing her by the washing with water through the word, and to present her to himself as a radiant church, without stain or wrinkle or any other blemish, but holy and blameless. In this same way, husbands ought to love their wives as their bodies. He who loves his wife loves himself."

Ephesians 6:1-4 (NIV): "Children, obey your parents in the Lord, for this is right. 'Honor your father and mother'—which is the first commandment with a promise—'so that it may go well with you and that you may enjoy long life on the earth.' Fathers, do not exasperate your children; instead, bring them up in the training and instruction of the Lord."

Elaboration:

Marital Love and Care: Ephesians 5:25-29 highlights the sacrificial and nurturing love husbands should have for their wives, mirroring Christ's love for the church. This deep, selfless love fosters a healthy, supportive marital relationship.

Parent-Child Relationships: Ephesians 6:1-4 emphasizes the importance of children obeying and honoring their parents, and parents (especially fathers) nurturing their children without provoking them. This creates a harmonious family environment rooted in respect and care.

Application:

Mutual Respect and Support: Foster family relationships based on mutual respect, love, and support. Husbands and wives should care for each other's well-being, and parents should provide loving guidance to their children.

Balanced Discipline and Nurturing: Parents should balance discipline with nurturing, ensuring children grow up in a supportive, faith-based environment that encourages their overall development.

1 Corinthians 6:19-20

1 Corinthians 6:19-20: Highlighting the Importance of Caring for One's Body as a Temple of the Holy Spirit

Verses:

1 Corinthians 6:19-20 (NIV): "Do you not know that your bodies are temples of the Holy Spirit, who is in you, whom you have received from God? You are not your; you were bought at a price. Therefore honor God with your bodies."

DOING THE DEVIL'S WORK BEHIND THE CHRISTIAN MASK

Elaboration:

Sacredness of the Body: These verses underscore the sanctity of the human body, as it is a dwelling place for the Holy Spirit. Caring for one's physical health is a personal and spiritual responsibility.

Holistic Health: Honoring God with one's body includes maintaining physical health, including proper nutrition, exercise, rest, and medical care when needed. This holistic approach to health aligns with spiritual well-being.

Application:

Self-Care as Spiritual Practice: View self-care activities, such as eating well, exercising, and getting adequate rest, as part of honoring God. This perspective encourages a balanced approach to health and spirituality.

Seek Medical Guidance: Do not hesitate to seek medical care when necessary. Acknowledging the role of healthcare in maintaining the body's well-being is a way of respecting and valuing the life and body given by God.

Balancing faith, family, and health is supported by critical biblical principles. By prioritizing love for God, fostering loving and respectful family relationships, and caring for one's body as a sacred temple, individuals can achieve a harmonious and fulfilling life that honors their spiritual, familial, and personal well-being. These biblical teachings provide a strong foundation for navigating the complexities of daily life while maintaining a deep and abiding faith.

In summary, choosing religion over family and health presents a delicate balance. Christianity teaches the importance of loving God above all. Still, it also emphasizes the significance of family and personal well-being. By integrating faith with family life, prioritizing health, and seeking a harmonious balance, believers can honor their religious commitments while nurturing their relationships and health. This approach leads to a more holistic and sustainable expression of faith, fostering spiritual growth and overall well-being.

Self-Awareness And Personal Responsibility

Lack Of Self-Awareness And Projection Of Personal Sins Onto Others

The lack of self-awareness and projection of personal sins onto others is a phenomenon that occurs when individuals fail to recognize or acknowledge their flaws, shortcomings, or moral failings, instead attributing those qualities to others. This concept explores the psychological mechanisms underlying this behavior, its implications for interpersonal relationships and community dynamics, and strategies for cultivating greater self-awareness and empathy.

Roots of Lack of Self-Awareness

Defense Mechanisms: Projection often serves as a defense mechanism, allowing individuals to avoid confronting uncomfortable truths about themselves by attributing negative traits or behaviors to others.

Denial and Rationalization: Individuals may deny or rationalize their faults, minimizing their significance or shifting blame onto external factors to protect their self-image or preserve their moral superiority.

Ego Protection: Ego-driven motivations, such as pride or insecurity, can fuel a lack of self-awareness, as individuals prioritize maintaining a positive self-image or reputation over engaging in genuine self-reflection or introspection.

Cognitive Biases: Cognitive biases, such as the fundamental attribution error or confirmation bias, may distort individuals' perceptions of themselves and others, reinforcing stereotypes or prejudices and hindering accurate self-assessment.

Manifestations of Projection

Judgment and Criticism: Individuals prone to projection may exhibit judgmental attitudes or harsh criticism towards others, projecting their insecurities or moral failings onto those they perceive as different or threatening.

Conflict and Defensiveness: Projection can escalate interpersonal conflict, as individuals become defensive or reactive when confronted with feedback or criticism that challenges their self-perception or worldview.

Scapegoating: In group settings, projection may lead to scapegoating, where individuals or marginalized groups are unfairly blamed or targeted to deflect attention from the collective group's failings or shortcomings.

Victim Mentality: Individuals who project their sins onto others may adopt a victim mentality, perceiving themselves as unjustly persecuted or oppressed while disregarding their role in perpetuating conflict or injustice.

Consequences of Lack of Self-Awareness and Projection

Strained Relationships: Projection can strain interpersonal relationships, eroding trust, empathy, and mutual understanding as individuals engage in blame-shifting or avoid taking responsibility for their actions.

Stagnation and Growth: Lack of self-awareness inhibits personal growth and development, as individuals remain stagnant or resistant to feedback and cannot acknowledge and address their areas for improvement.

Community Division: Projection can contribute to division within communities or society, fostering an us-vs-them mentality that reinforces stereotypes, prejudices, and social polarization.

Spiritual Stagnation: In a religious context, lack of self-awareness and projection hinder spiritual growth and moral development, as individuals prioritize outward displays of piety or righteousness over inner transformation and humility.

Cultivating Self-Awareness and Empathy

Reflection and Introspection: Encouraging individuals to reflect and introspection fosters greater self-awareness, inviting them to explore their thoughts, emotions, and behaviors with honesty and curiosity.

Active Listening: Practicing active listening and empathic communication enables individuals to understand others' perspectives and experiences better, fostering empathy and compassion in their interactions.

Feedback and Accountability: Providing constructive feedback and accountability structures within communities encourages individuals to confront their blind spots and areas for growth, promoting personal and communal transformation.

Cultivating Humility: Cultivating humility as a virtue emphasizes the importance of acknowledging one's limitations, recognizing the humanity and dignity of others, and embracing a posture of openness and receptivity to feedback and learning.

In summary, the lack of self-awareness and projection of personal sins onto others reflect complex psychological dynamics that can undermine interpersonal relationships, community cohesion, and spiritual growth. Individuals can break free from the projection cycle by cultivating greater self-awareness, empathy, and humility, fostering deeper connections, mutual respect, and collective flourishing within religious communities and society.

The Importance Of Personal Accountability In Spiritual Growth

Personal accountability is crucial in spiritual growth as a cornerstone for individuals' development and maturation within their faith journey. This concept explores the significance of personal responsibility in fostering spiritual growth, its implications for individual and communal well-being, and practical strategies for cultivating accountability within religious communities.

Foundations of Personal Accountability

Self-Reflection: Personal accountability begins with self-reflection, as individuals engage in introspection to examine their beliefs, values, and behaviors and assess their alignment with their spiritual aspirations and commitments.

Ownership of Actions: Personal accountability entails owning one's actions, choices, and decisions, recognizing their impact on oneself, others, and the broader community, and accepting responsibility for consequences.

Commitment to Growth: Accountability involves a commitment to growth and improvement as individuals strive to learn from their mistakes, address their shortcomings, and pursue ongoing personal and spiritual development.

Alignment with Values: Personal accountability requires aligning one's actions with one's professed values and principles, ensuring consistency between one's beliefs and behaviors to foster integrity and authenticity in one's spiritual life.

Role of Personal Accountability in Spiritual Growth

Self-Awareness: Personal accountability fosters self-awareness, enabling individuals to identify areas for growth and transformation in their spiritual journey and to confront their limitations, biases, and blind spots.

Integrity and Authenticity: Accountability promotes integrity and authenticity in one's spiritual practice as individuals strive to live following their deepest values and convictions, cultivating a sense of wholeness and coherence in their identity and purpose.

Empowerment: Taking personal accountability empowers individuals to actively shape their spiritual path and destiny rather than passively relying on external forces or circumstances, fostering a sense of agency and autonomy in their relationship with the divine.

Resilience: Accountability builds resilience in the face of adversity or setbacks as individuals learn to persevere in their spiritual journey, navigate challenges with grace and perseverance, and bounce back from failures or disappointments with renewed determination and faith.

Relational Growth: Personal accountability contributes to relational growth and community cohesion, as individuals model integrity, humility, and vulnerability in their interactions with others, fostering trust, mutual respect, and collaborative efforts towards shared spiritual goals.

Cultivating Personal Accountability

Goal Setting: Setting clear, achievable goals and intentions for spiritual growth provides a roadmap for personal accountability, guiding individuals to cultivate specific virtues, practices, or qualities.

Accountability Partners: Establishing accountability partnerships or mentorship relationships with trusted peers or spiritual guides offers support, encouragement, and feedback in one's personal growth and accountability journey.

Reflection Practices: Engaging in regular reflection practices, such as journaling, meditation, or spiritual retreats, provides opportunities for self-examination, discernment, and course correction in response to insights gained from contemplative practices.

Community Engagement: Active participation in religious communities or spiritual groups fosters accountability through shared rituals, collective worship, and mutual accountability structures that encourage individuals to uphold their commitments and support one another in their spiritual aspirations.

Learning from Failure: Embracing failure as an opportunity for learning and growth cultivates resilience and humility as individuals confront their mistakes, seek forgiveness and reconciliation where necessary, and emerge stronger and wiser from their experiences.

Personal accountability is indispensable for spiritual growth, empowering individuals to navigate their spiritual journey with integrity, authenticity, and resilience. By embracing accountability as a guiding principle, individuals can foster deeper self-awareness, relational growth, and transformative change, leading to a more fulfilling and purposeful engagement with their faith and community.

Examination Of The Impact Of Self-Hate On Interpersonal Relationships

The impact of self-hate on interpersonal relationships is profound, affecting not only the individual experiencing it but also those with whom they interact. This examination delves into how self-hate can manifest in relationships, its detrimental effects on communication, trust, and intimacy, and strategies for addressing and mitigating its impact on interpersonal dynamics.

Manifestations of Self-Hate in Interpersonal Relationships

Low Self-Esteem: Individuals experiencing self-hate may struggle with low self-esteem, viewing themselves as unworthy or unlovable, which can manifest in seeking validation or approval from others or engaging in self-sabotaging behaviors.

Insecurity and Jealousy: Self-hate often leads to insecurity and jealousy in relationships, as individuals compare themselves unfavorably to others, fear rejection or abandonment, or perceive themselves as inadequate or inferior.

Emotional Withdrawal: Some individuals may withdraw emotionally in relationships, fearing vulnerability or intimacy and erecting emotional barriers or defenses to protect themselves from perceived rejection or criticism.

People-Pleasing: Individuals may engage in people-pleasing behaviors, sacrificing their needs or boundaries to gain acceptance or avoid conflict. This leads to resentment or codependency in relationships.

Dysfunctional Patterns: Self-hate can perpetuate dysfunctional relationship patterns, such as passive-aggressive behavior, manipulation, or emotional dependency, as individuals struggle to navigate their insecurities and self-doubts.

Effects of Self-Hate on Interpersonal Dynamics

Communication Breakd: Self-hate can impair relationships, leading to misunderstandings, misinterpretations, or defensiveness as individuals struggle to express their needs, feelings, or boundaries authentically.

Trust Issues: Individuals experiencing self-hate may have difficulty trusting others, fearing rejection or betrayal, and interpreting benign actions or gestures as signs of disapproval or abandonment, undermining the foundation of trust in their relationships.

Conflict Avoidance: Self-hate often leads to conflict avoidance in relationships, as individuals fear confrontation or rejection and prioritize maintaining harmony at the expense of addressing underlying issues or tensions.

Emotional Distance: Self-hate can create emotional distance or detachment in relationships, as individuals struggle to connect authentically with others and may withhold vulnerability or intimacy out of fear of rejection or judgment.

Impact on Intimacy: Self-hate can hinder intimacy in relationships, as individuals struggle to accept love or affection from others, feeling unworthy or undeserving of closeness, and may sabotage or undermine intimate connections.

Addressing Self-Hate in Interpersonal Relationships

Self-Compassion: Cultivating self-compassion is essential for addressing self-hate, as individuals learn to treat themselves with kindness, understanding, and acceptance, recognizing their inherent worth and dignity regardless of perceived flaws or shortcomings.

Therapeutic Support: Seeking therapeutic support can help individuals address underlying issues contributing to self-hate, such as trauma, negative self-talk, or distorted beliefs, and develop healthier coping strategies and self-esteem.

Boundaries and Assertiveness: Establishing and maintaining healthy boundaries is crucial for navigating relationships with self-hate, as individuals learn to assert their needs, preferences, and limits assertively, fostering mutual respect and authenticity in their interactions.

Communication Skills: Improving communication skills, such as active listening, empathy, and assertive expression, enhances interpersonal relationships by fostering understanding, trust, and emotional connection with others.

Mindfulness Practices: Engaging in mindfulness practices, such as meditation or journaling, promotes self-awareness and emotional regulation, helping individuals recognize and manage self-hate triggers and cultivate a greater sense of inner peace and resilience.

In summary, the impact of self-hate on interpersonal relationships is significant, affecting communication, trust, intimacy, and overall relationship dynamics. By addressing self-hate with self-compassion, therapeutic support, boundary-setting, communication skills, and mindfulness practices, individuals can cultivate healthier, more fulfilling relationships characterized by authenticity, empathy, and mutual respect.

Ask Yourself, How Self-Aware Are You?

Asking oneself about their level of self-awareness is a crucial aspect of personal growth and development. It prompts individuals to reflect on their understanding of themselves, emotions, thoughts, and behaviors and consider how this awareness impacts their relationships, decision-making, and overall well-being.

Here are some key points to consider when exploring this question:

Understanding Self-Awareness: Reflect on what self-awareness means to you. How do you define it, and why do you consider it essential?

Examining Inner Thoughts and Feelings: Consider how in tune you are with your inner thoughts, emotions, and reactions. Can you recognize and name your feelings as they arise, and do you understand the underlying reasons for those feelings?

Observing External Reactions: Reflect on how you perceive and interpret the reactions of others towards you. Do you know how your words and actions impact those around you, and do you take responsibility for your effects on others?

Exploring Personal Strengths and Weaknesses: Evaluate your awareness of your strengths, weaknesses, and areas for growth. Are you honest about your limitations and areas where you need improvement, and do you actively work towards personal development?

Assessing Behavior Patterns: Consider whether you recognize and understand patterns in your behavior. Can you identify recurring patterns or habits that may be hindering your progress or causing you distress, and do you take steps to address them?

Cultivating Mindfulness: Reflect on your ability to stay present and mindful in everyday life. Can you fully engage with the present moment, or are you distracted or preoccupied with thoughts of the past or future?

Seeking Feedback: Consider how open you are to receiving feedback from others about yourself. Are you receptive to constructive criticism and willing to consider different perspectives, or do you become defensive or dismissive when faced with feedback?

Embracing Vulnerability: Reflect on your willingness to embrace vulnerability and explore your innermost thoughts and feelings. Are you comfortable being vulnerable with yourself and others, or do you tend to avoid discomfort by suppressing or denying difficult emotions?

Practicing Reflection: Evaluate how often you engage in self-reflection and introspection. Do you set aside time regularly to reflect on your experiences, learnings, and goals, or do you tend to move through life without pausing to consider your inner world?

Committing to Growth: Consider your attitude towards personal growth and self-improvement. Are you proactive in seeking opportunities for growth and learning, or do you resist change and cling to familiar ways of thinking and behaving?

By asking oneself about their level of self-awareness, individuals can deepen their understanding of themselves and their relationship to the world around them. This introspective inquiry can lead to greater self-acceptance, emotional resilience, and authenticity in interactions and pursuits.

The Lark Code And Self-Improvement

Application Of The Lark Code To Christian Values And Behavior

Applying the LARK Code to Christian values and behavior offers a transformative approach to living out the teachings of Jesus Christ with authenticity, compassion, and integrity. By integrating the principles of Love, Acceptance, Respect, and Know Yourself into their spiritual journey, Christians can deepen their relationship with God, foster meaningful connections with others, and embody the essence of Christ's message of love, grace, and inclusion.

Love Yourself

Love as the Greatest Commandment: Embracing the principle of Love aligns with Jesus' teaching that the greatest commandment is to love God with all one's heart, soul, and mind and to love one's neighbor as oneself (Matthew 22:37-40).

Unconditional Love and Forgiveness: Practicing Love involves extending unconditional love and forgiveness towards oneself and others, mirroring God's boundless love and grace toward humanity, as exemplified in Jesus' life and teachings.

Radical Hospitality: Love inspires Christians to embody radical hospitality, welcoming the stranger, the outcast, and the marginalized with open arms and creating inclusive communities where all are valued and affirmed.

Accept Yourself

Embrace of Diversity: Acceptance reflects Jesus' embrace of diversity and inclusion, as he welcomed sinners, tax collectors, and social outcasts into his fellowship, challenging societal norms and prejudices (Luke 5:27-32).

Non-Judgmental Attitude: Practicing Acceptance involves adopting a non-judgmental attitude toward others, refraining from condemnation or exclusion, and recognizing every individual's inherent worth and dignity as a beloved child of God.

Redemption and Restoration: Acceptance acknowledges the possibility of redemption and transformation in every person, extending grace and compassion to those who have fallen short and creating opportunities for healing and reconciliation.

Respect Yourself

Dignity of Every Person: Respect affirms the dignity and worth of every person as a divine creation, made in the image of God, and calls Christians to treat others with reverence, honor, and humility (Genesis 1:27).

Listening and Understanding: Practicing Respect involves listening attentively to others' experiences, perspectives, and needs, seeking to understand and validate their journey, and honoring their autonomy, agency, and worth.

Servant Leadership: Respect exemplifies Jesus' servant leadership model, as he humbly washed his disciples' feet, demonstrating that true greatness comes from serving others with humility and love (John 13:1-17).

Know Yourself

Identity in Christ: Know Yourself encourages Christians to discover their identity and purpose in Christ, rooted in their relationship with God as beloved children, redeemed by grace, and called to live out their faith with authenticity and integrity (Galatians 2:20).

Spiritual Discernment: Practicing Know Yourself involves cultivating spiritual discernment and wisdom, deepening one's understanding of God's will and guidance, and aligning one's thoughts, desires, and actions with God's truth and love.

Holistic Growth: Know Yourself fosters holistic growth and maturity, as Christians seek to know themselves more fully—spiritually, emotionally, and relationally—and to align with their values, convictions, and calling in every area of life.

Application in Christian Life

Prayer and Reflection: Christians can apply the LARK Code through prayer, meditation, and reflection, seeking God's guidance and empowerment to embody Love, Acceptance, Respect, and Know Yourself in their daily lives and relationships.

Community Engagement: Christians can practice the LARK Code in their interactions with fellow believers and the broader community, fostering inclusive and compassionate communities that reflect the transformative power of Christ's love and grace.

Social Justice and Advocacy: Christians can advocate for justice, equality, and dignity for all, addressing systemic injustices and inequalities that undermine the principles of Love, Acceptance, Respect, and Know Yourself, and working towards a more just and equitable society.

In summary, applying the LARK Code to Christian values and behavior offers a transformative framework for living out the essence of Christ's teachings with authenticity, compassion, and integrity. By embracing Love, Acceptance, Respect, and Know Yourself, Christians can deepen their relationship with God, cultivate meaningful connections with others, and witness the transformative power of Christ's love and grace in their lives and communities.

Proposition Of A Path To Personal And Collective Improvement

The proposition of a path to personal and collective improvement involves identifying fundamental principles and practices that individuals and communities can embrace to foster growth, well-being, and positive transformation. This path integrates self-awareness, empathy, collaboration, and resilience, empowering individuals and groups to navigate challenges, pursue goals, and contribute to the greater good. Here's an elaboration on each component:

Self-Awareness

Reflection and Introspection: Cultivating self-awareness begins with reflection and introspection, as individuals explore their thoughts, emotions, and behaviors with honesty and curiosity, gaining insight into their strengths, weaknesses, and areas for growth.

Mindfulness Practices: Engaging in mindfulness practices, such as meditation or journaling, promotes present-moment awareness and emotional regulation, helping individuals develop greater clarity, focus, and resilience in navigating life's challenges.

Feedback and Self-Reflection: Seeking input from trusted sources and reflecting on one's experiences and interactions provides opportunities for learning and growth as individuals gain perspective on their actions, impact, and areas for improvement.

Empathy and Connection

Active Listening and Understanding: Practicing empathy involves active listening and understanding, seeking to understand others' perspectives, experiences, and needs with compassion and openness, and validating their feelings and concerns.

Compassionate Communication: Communicating with empathy and compassion fosters deeper connections and trust in relationships as individuals express care, understanding, and support for others, creating a safe space for vulnerability and authenticity.

Cultivation of Empathy: Cultivating empathy involves stepping into others' shoes, recognizing their humanity and dignity, and extending grace and kindness towards them, even in moments of disagreement or conflict.

Collaboration and Community

Shared Goals and Values: Collaboration thrives on shared goals and values, as individuals and groups come together around a common purpose or vision, pooling their talents, resources, and perspectives to achieve collective objectives.

Strength in Diversity: Embracing diversity and inclusion enriches collaboration, as individuals with different backgrounds, perspectives, and skills contribute unique insights and ideas, fostering innovation, creativity, and resilience in problem-solving and decision-making.

Supportive Networks and Relationships: Building supportive networks and relationships strengthens community bonds as individuals offer encouragement, accountability, and mutual aid to one another, creating a culture of care, belonging, and reciprocity.

Resilience and Growth Mindset

Adaptability and Flexibility: Resilience involves adaptability and flexibility in the face of change or adversity, as individuals embrace challenges as opportunities for learning, growth, and innovation and bounce back from setbacks with renewed determination and optimism.

Optimism and Positive Framing: Cultivating a growth mindset fosters optimism and a positive framing of challenges, as individuals focus on solutions, possibilities, and strengths rather than dwelling on limitations or failures and maintaining hope and possibility in uncertain times.

Self-Care and Well-Being: Prioritizing self-care and well-being sustains resilience and prevents burnout, as individuals attend to their physical, emotional, and spiritual needs and cultivate practices that promote balance, restoration, and renewal.

Collective Action and Impact

Shared Responsibility: Collective improvement requires shared responsibility and accountability, as individuals and communities recognize their interconnectedness and interdependence and work collaboratively towards common goals and values.

Empowerment and Agency: Empowering individuals to take initiative and lead creates a sense of agency and ownership in driving change as individuals identify opportunities for action, mobilize resources, and advocate for solutions that address shared challenges and aspirations.

Celebration of Progress: Celebrating progress and milestones fosters a sense of accomplishment and momentum as individuals and communities acknowledge and honor their achievements and draw inspiration and motivation from their collective efforts and successes.

In summary, the proposition of a path to personal and collective improvement offers a comprehensive framework for fostering growth, well-being, and positive transformation at the individual and community levels. By embracing self-awareness, empathy, collaboration, resilience, and collective action, individuals and groups can navigate challenges, cultivate meaningful connections, and contribute to the greater good, creating a more just, equitable, and thriving world for all.

Becoming A Better Christian Through The Lark Code

Embracing the LARK Code—Love, Acceptance, Respect, Know Yourself—offers a transformative pathway for individuals seeking to deepen their Christian faith and embody the teachings of Jesus Christ with authenticity, compassion, and integrity. By integrating the principles of the LARK Code into their spiritual journey, Christians can cultivate a deeper relationship with God, foster meaningful connections with others, and witness the transformative power of Christ's love and grace in their lives and communities. Here's an elaboration on how one can become a better Christian through the LARK Code:

Love (Love Yourself and Others)

Love as the Greatest Commandment: Embrace the principle of Love as Jesus taught, recognizing it as the greatest commandment—to love God with all your heart, soul, and mind, and to love your neighbor as yourself (Matthew 22:37-40).

Self-Love and Self-Compassion: Practice self-love and self-compassion, recognizing your inherent worth and belovedness as a child of God and extending grace, kindness, and forgiveness towards yourself in moments of struggle or imperfection.

Radical Hospitality: Embody radical hospitality by welcoming others with open arms, regardless of their background, beliefs, or circumstances, and creating inclusive communities where all are valued, accepted, and affirmed.

Acceptance (Accept Yourself and Others)

Embrace Diversity: Practice Acceptance by embracing diversity and inclusion, recognizing the inherent dignity and worth of every individual as a beloved creation of God, and celebrating the richness of human experiences, identities, and perspectives.

Non-Judgmental Attitude: Cultivate a non-judgmental attitude towards others, refraining from condemnation or exclusion and extending grace, compassion, and understanding to those different from you, just as Jesus did.

Redemption and Restoration: Belief in the possibility of redemption and transformation in every person, extending grace and compassion to those who have fallen short and creating opportunities for healing, reconciliation, and restoration in relationships and communities.

Respect (Respect Yourself and Others)

The dignity of Every Person: Honor the dignity and worth of every person as a divine creation, made in the image of God, and treat others with reverence, honor, and humility, recognizing the sacredness of their humanity.

Listening and Understanding: Practice Respect by listening attentively to others' experiences, perspectives, and needs, seeking to understand and validate their journey, and honoring their autonomy, agency, and worth in all interactions.

Servant Leadership: Embody servant leadership by humbly serving others with love and compassion, following Jesus' example of washing his disciples' feet, and prioritizing the needs and well-being of others above your own.

Know Yourself (and Others)

Identity in Christ: Discover your identity and purpose in Christ, rooted in your relationship with God as a beloved child, redeemed by grace, and called to live out your faith with authenticity, integrity, and courage.

Spiritual Discernment: Cultivate spiritual discernment and wisdom, deepening your understanding of God's will and guidance and aligning your thoughts, desires, and actions with God's truth and love.

Holistic Growth: Pursue holistic growth and maturity, seeking to know yourself more fully—spiritually, emotionally, and relationally—and to live in alignment with your values, convictions, and calling in every area of life.

Application in Christian Life

Prayer and Reflection: Apply the LARK Code through prayer, meditation, and reflection, seeking God's guidance and empowerment to embody Love, Acceptance, Respect, and Know Yourself in your daily life and relationships.

Community Engagement: Practice the LARK Code in your interactions with fellow believers and the broader community, fostering inclusive and compassionate communities that reflect the transformative power of Christ's love and grace.

Social Justice and Advocacy: Advocate for justice, equality, and dignity for all, addressing systemic injustices and inequalities that undermine the principles of Love, Acceptance, Respect, and Know Yourself, and working towards a more just and equitable society.

In summary, becoming a better Christian through the LARK Code involves embracing principles of Love, Acceptance, Respect, and Know Yourself as foundational values for spiritual growth, relational harmony, and collective transformation. By integrating these principles into their faith journey and daily life, Christians can deepen their relationship with God, cultivate meaningful connections with others, and bear witness to the transformative power of Christ's love and grace in their lives and communities.

Ask Yourself, Do You Follow The Lark Code?

Asking oneself whether they follow the LARK Code is an invitation to reflect on their commitment to living a life guided by Love, Acceptance, Respect, and Knowing oneself. The LARK Code serves as a framework for fostering self-awareness, empathy, and compassion towards oneself and others. Here's a breakdown of each component of the LARK Code and what it entails:

Love: Reflect on how you demonstrate love in daily interactions and relationships. Do you show kindness, empathy, and compassion towards yourself and others? Can you cultivate a deep love and appreciation for yourself, recognizing your worth and inherent value as a human being?

Acceptance: Consider your attitude towards acceptance and inclusivity. Can you accept yourself and others as they are, without judgment or prejudice? Do you embrace diversity and celebrate the uniqueness of each individual, recognizing that differences enrich our shared humanity?

Respect: Reflect on how you demonstrate respect for yourself and others. Do you treat yourself and others with dignity, kindness, and consideration? Are you mindful of boundaries and consent, honoring the autonomy and agency of each person?

Know Yourself: Consider your level of self-awareness and introspection. Do you take the time to explore your thoughts, feelings, and motivations? Are you aware of your strengths, weaknesses, and values, and do you strive to live in alignment with your authentic self?

By asking themselves whether they follow the LARK Code, individuals can assess their adherence to these principles and identify areas for growth and improvement. This introspective inquiry can lead to greater self-awareness, empathy, and alignment with one's values, ultimately fostering deeper connections and a more meaningful and fulfilling life.

Genuine Faith Vs. Hypocrisy

Discerning Genuine Faith From Hypocrisy

Discerning genuine faith from hypocrisy requires a nuanced understanding of the outward expressions and the inner motivations of individuals claiming to adhere to a particular belief system, such as Christianity. While outward behaviors and expressions may indicate a person's faith, true discernment often lies in examining the consistency between professed beliefs and lived values and the sincerity of one's intentions and actions. Here's an elaboration on how to discern genuine faith from hypocrisy:

Consistency Between Beliefs and Actions

Lived Values: Genuine faith is characterized by consistency between one's professed beliefs and lived values, as individuals strive to embody the teachings and principles of their faith in their daily lives, relationships, and actions.

Integrity and Authenticity: Genuine faith is marked by integrity and authenticity as individuals demonstrate transparency, honesty, and sincerity in their words and deeds, aligning their actions with their professed beliefs without pretense or hypocrisy.

Fruit of the Spirit: Genuine faith produces "fruit of the Spirit," such as love, joy, peace, patience, kindness, goodness, faithfulness, gentleness, and self-control (Galatians 5:22-23), manifesting in positive attitudes, behaviors, and interactions with others.

Humility and Self-Reflection

Humility: Genuine faith is characterized by humility, as individuals acknowledge their imperfections, limitations, and need for growth and approach others with humility, openness, and a willingness to learn and grow.

Self-Reflection: Genuine faith involves ongoing self-reflection and examination of one's beliefs, attitudes, and actions as individuals humbly seek to discern areas of growth, repentance, and transformation in their spiritual journey.

Compassion and Empathy

Compassion: Genuine faith is marked by compassion and empathy towards others, as individuals extend grace, mercy, and kindness to those in need, reflecting the love and compassion of God as expressed through Jesus Christ.

Empathy: Genuine faith involves empathizing with others' experiences, perspectives, and struggles as individuals seek to understand and validate the feelings and needs of others with compassion, sensitivity, and understanding.

Fruitful Relationships and Community Engagement

Authentic Relationships: Genuine faith fosters authentic relationships built on trust, mutual respect, and genuine care for one another as individuals nurture meaningful connections and support one another in their spiritual journey.

Community Engagement: Genuine faith is demonstrated through active engagement and participation in communities of faith, as individuals contribute their time, talents, and resources to the well-being and flourishing of the community and work collaboratively towards common goals and values.

In summary, discerning genuine faith from hypocrisy requires careful examination of outward behaviors and inner motivations and considering factors such as consistency between beliefs and actions, humility and self-reflection, compassion and empathy, and fruitful relationships and community engagement. By cultivating discernment and wisdom, individuals can distinguish between authentic expressions of faith and mere outward appearances and strive to embody genuine faith characterized by integrity, humility, compassion, and love.

Exploration Of Motivations Behind Religious Practices

Exploring the motivations behind religious practices reveals a complex interplay of personal, cultural, and spiritual factors that shape individuals' beliefs, behaviors, and sense of identity within their religious tradition. These motivations vary widely among individuals and may include a combination of intrinsic and extrinsic factors and a deep sense of meaning, belonging, and connection to something greater than oneself. Here's an elaboration on the motivations behind religious practices:

Spiritual Fulfillment and Connection

Seeking Meaning and Purpose: Many individuals engage in religious practices as a means of seeking meaning, purpose, and fulfillment in life, finding solace, guidance, and a sense of transcendence in their spiritual beliefs and practices.

Deepening Connection with the Divine: Religious practices offer opportunities for individuals to deepen their connection with the divine or spiritual realm, fostering a sense of intimacy, communion, and reverence in their relationship with God, the sacred, or the transcendent.

Expressing Devotion and Gratitude: Religious practices provide avenues for expressing devotion, gratitude, and reverence towards the divine, as individuals offer prayers, rituals, and acts of worship as expressions of their faith and devotion.

Cultural and Social Influences

Cultural Identity and Heritage: Religious practices often reflect individuals' cultural identity and heritage, serving as a means of preserving traditions, values, and customs passed d through generations and fostering a sense of belonging and continuity within a cultural community.

Social Bonds and Community: Religious practices foster social bonds and community cohesion as individuals gather for worship, fellowship, and communal rituals, forging meaningful connections and relationships with others who share their faith and values.

Moral and Ethical Framework: Religious practices provide a moral and ethical framework for individuals to navigate life's challenges and dilemmas, offering guidance, support, and accountability in upholding shared values and principles within their religious community.

Personal Growth and Transformation

Spiritual Growth and Enlightenment: Religious practices facilitate personal growth and spiritual enlightenment as individuals engage in prayer, meditation, study, and reflection to deepen their understanding of spiritual truths, cultivate virtues, and transcend the limitations of the ego.

Healing and Wholeness: Religious practices offer avenues for healing and wholeness, addressing spiritual, emotional, and psychological needs and providing comfort, solace, and hope in times of suffering, loss, or adversity.

Transformation and Redemption: Religious practices promote personal transformation and redemption as individuals seek forgiveness, reconciliation, and renewal through repentance, atonement, and spiritual discipline and strive to align with their highest ideals and values.

In summary, the motivations behind religious practices are multifaceted and deeply intertwined with individuals' spiritual, cultural, and social identities. Whether seeking spiritual fulfillment and connection, expressing cultural heritage and identity, fostering social bonds and community, or pursuing personal growth and transformation, individuals engage in religious practices as a means of seeking meaning, purpose, and fulfillment in life and cultivating a deeper relationship with the divine, themselves, and others. By understanding these motivations, we can gain insight into the rich tapestry of human spirituality and how individuals express their faith and beliefs within the context of their religious tradition.

Consequences Of Using Religion As A Mask For Immoral Behavior

Using religion as a mask for immoral behavior can have profound and far-reaching consequences, both for individuals and for the wider community. This practice not only distorts the true essence of religion but also undermines the trust, integrity, and moral fabric of society. Here's an elaboration on the consequences of using religion as a mask for immoral behavior:

Erosion of Trust and Credibility

Loss of Trust in Religious Institutions: When individuals misuse religion to justify immoral behavior, trust in religious institutions and leaders erodes, undermining their credibility and authority as moral guides and spiritual authorities.

Betrayal of Trust: Using religion as a mask for immoral behavior betrays the trust of believers who look to religious leaders and institutions for moral guidance and ethical leadership, leading to disillusionment, skepticism, and cynicism towards religion.

Damage to Reputation: Individuals who exploit religion for personal gain or to conceal wrongdoing risk damaging their reputation and credibility, tarnishing the reputation of their religious community and faith tradition in the process.

Hypocrisy and Inconsistency

Hypocrisy: Using religion as a mask for immoral behavior perpetuates hypocrisy, as individuals espouse one set of beliefs or values publicly while privately engaging in behavior that contradicts those beliefs, leading to a disconnect between professed faith and lived actions.

Inconsistency: This inconsistency between professed beliefs and actions undermines religious practice's moral integrity and authenticity, diminishing its transformative power and relevance in individuals' lives and communities.

Loss of Moral Authority: Hypocritical behavior weakens the moral authority of religious leaders and institutions, as it exposes the gap between their words and deeds, undermining their ability to advocate for ethical principles and social justice effectively.

Harm to Individuals and Communities

Exploitation and Abuse: Using religion as a mask for immoral behavior can result in the exploitation and abuse of vulnerable individuals, as religious leaders or authorities misuse their power and influence to manipulate, control, or harm others for personal gain.

Psychological Harm: Individuals who experience or witness hypocrisy and moral misconduct within religious communities may suffer psychological harm, including feelings of betrayal, shame, and disillusionment, leading to spiritual, emotional, and psychological distress.

Division and Conflict: Hypocrisy and moral misconduct within religious communities can lead to division, conflict, and fragmentation as individuals grapple with conflicting interpretations of spiritual teachings and values and struggle to reconcile their faith with the actions of those who misuse it.

Loss of Spiritual Meaning and Purpose

Spiritual Emptiness: Using religion as a mask for immoral behavior creates a sense of spiritual emptiness and disconnection, as individuals prioritize external rituals and appearances over inner transformation and moral integrity, leading to a shallow and superficial understanding of religion.

Loss of Meaning and Purpose: Individuals who misuse religion for selfish or nefarious purposes risk losing sight of its more profound meaning and purpose as they prioritize personal gain or status over pursuing spiritual growth, ethical conduct, and service to others.

Alienation from God: Hypocritical behavior alienates individuals from God or their spiritual beliefs, as they experience guilt, shame, or spiritual conflict arising from the disparity between their professed faith and lived actions, hindering their ability to experience true peace, joy, and fulfillment in their spiritual journey.

In summary, the consequences of using religion as a mask for immoral behavior are manifold and profound, ranging from erosion of trust and credibility to perpetuation of hypocrisy and inconsistency, harm to individuals and communities, and loss of spiritual meaning and purpose. By recognizing and addressing these consequences, individuals and communities can strive to uphold religious practice's integrity, authenticity, and transformative power and cultivate a more profound commitment to ethical conduct, moral integrity, and genuine spirituality within their religious tradition.

Ask Yourself, Are You Faithful Or A Hypocrite?

Asking oneself whether they are faithful or a hypocrite is a probing question that delves into the alignment between one's professed beliefs and their actions. Here's a breakdown of each aspect of this question:

Faithfulness: Reflect on your commitment to your beliefs and values. Are you faithful in living according to the principles and teachings that you claim to uphold? Do you strive to embody the virtues of your faith in your daily life, demonstrating integrity, honesty, and sincerity in your actions?

Hypocrisy: Consider whether there are inconsistencies between your beliefs and your behavior. Do you profess certain beliefs or moral standards but fail to live up to them in practice? Are there instances where you act in ways that contradict your stated values or principles?

Individuals can engage in honest self-reflection and evaluate the congruence between their beliefs and actions by asking themselves whether they are faithful or hypocritical. This introspective inquiry can catalyze personal growth and transformation, empowering individuals to align their behavior more closely with their professed values and live authentically following their faith.

Recapitulation Of Central Arguments

In recapitulating the central arguments, it's essential to highlight the key points and insights discussed throughout the exploration. Here's a concise recap of the central arguments:

The LARK Code as a Framework: The LARK Code—Love, Acceptance, Respect, Know Yourself—provides a transformative framework for personal and relational growth rooted in principles of self-love, acceptance, respect, and self-awareness, which align with the core tenets of Christianity.

Genuine Faith vs. Hypocrisy: Discerning genuine faith from hypocrisy involves examining the consistency between professed beliefs and lived values, the sincerity of one's intentions and actions, and the alignment with the teachings and example of Jesus Christ.

Motivations Behind Religious Practices: The motivations behind religious practices are multifaceted, encompassing spiritual fulfillment, cultural identity, social bonds, personal growth, and transformation, reflecting individuals' quest for meaning, connection, and transcendence within their religious tradition.

Consequences of Misusing Religion: Using religion as a mask for immoral behavior can lead to erosion of trust and credibility in religious institutions, perpetuation of hypocrisy and inconsistency, harm to individuals and communities, and loss of spiritual meaning and purpose, undermining the integrity and authenticity of religious practice.

Call to Authenticity and Integrity: In light of these insights, there is a call to embrace authenticity and integrity in our faith journey, to cultivate genuine love, acceptance, respect, and self-awareness in our interactions with ourselves and others, and to uphold the transformative power of religious practice in promoting personal and collective well-being.

By recapitulating these central arguments, we reaffirm the importance of living authentically and embodying the values of love, acceptance, respect, and self-awareness in our spiritual journey, fostering deeper connections, meaningful growth, and positive transformation in our lives and communities.

Call To Action For Self-Reflection And Genuine Spiritual Growth.

The call to action for self-reflection and genuine spiritual growth is an invitation to embark on a transformative journey of inner exploration, self-discovery, and personal development rooted in authenticity, integrity, and spiritual depth. Here's an elaboration on this call to action:

Self-Reflection

Pause and Contemplate: Take time to pause and contemplate your beliefs, values, and actions, reflecting on the alignment between your professed faith and lived experience and identifying areas for growth and transformation.

Question Assumptions: Challenge assumptions and beliefs based on cultural conditioning, societal norms, or personal biases, and engage in critical self-inquiry to deepen your understanding of your faith and its implications for your life.

Seek Feedback: Seek feedback from trusted mentors, peers, or spiritual guides, inviting them to provide insights and perspectives on your spiritual journey and offering opportunities for growth and learning through dialogue and reflection.

Genuine Spiritual Growth

Cultivate Inner Awareness: Cultivate inner awareness and mindfulness through practices such as meditation, prayer, or journaling, nurturing a deeper connection with your innermost self and with the divine presence within and around you.

Embrace Vulnerability: Embrace vulnerability as a pathway to growth and transformation, allowing yourself to be open and receptive to new insights, experiences, and challenges that may arise in your spiritual journey.

Practice Compassion: Practice compassion towards yourself and others, extending grace, kindness, and understanding in moments of struggle or imperfection and fostering an environment of acceptance and support in your relationships and community.

Authentic Living

Align with Values: Align your beliefs, values, and actions with integrity, striving to live authentically and congruently with your deepest convictions and aspirations and embodying the principles of love, acceptance, respect, and self-awareness in all aspects of your life.

Be a Lifelong Learner: Embrace a mindset of curiosity and lifelong learning, remaining open to new ideas, perspectives, and experiences that challenge and inspire you to deepen your understanding of yourself, others, and the divine mysteries of existence.

Engage in Service: Engage in acts of service and compassion that extend beyond yourself, contributing your time, talents, and resources to uplift and empower those in need and cultivating a spirit of generosity, humility, and empathy in your interactions with others.

In summary, the call to action for self-reflection and genuine spiritual growth invites you to embark on a journey of inner exploration, self-discovery, and personal development that empowers you to live authentically, align with your values, and cultivate deeper connections with yourself, others, and the divine. By embracing this call to action, you can nurture a sense of meaning, purpose, and fulfillment in your spiritual journey and contribute to the greater good by embodying the transformative power of love, acceptance, respect, and self-awareness in your life and relationships.

Vision For A More Compassionate And Authentic Expression Of Christianity

The vision for a more compassionate and authentic expression of Christianity envisions a faith community that embodies the teachings and example of Jesus Christ with integrity, humility, and love, fostering a culture of compassion, inclusivity, and genuine spiritual growth. Here's an elaboration on this vision:

Compassionate Community

Radical Love and Acceptance: Embrace a culture of radical love and acceptance where all individuals are welcomed, valued, and affirmed regardless of their background, beliefs, or circumstances, fostering a sense of belonging and dignity for all.

Empathy and Compassion: Cultivate empathy and compassion in all interactions, seeking to understand and validate the experiences, feelings, and needs of others with sensitivity, kindness, and care, and offering support and solidarity in times of struggle or adversity.

Service and Social Justice: Engage in acts of service and social justice that address systemic injustices and inequalities, advocating for the rights and dignity of the marginalized and vulnerable and working towards a more just, equitable, and compassionate society.

Authentic Spiritual Growth

Integrity and Authenticity: Embody integrity and authenticity in your faith journey, aligning your beliefs, values, and actions with honesty, transparency, and sincerity and cultivating a deeper relationship with God and with yourself through practices of prayer, meditation, and self-reflection.

Vulnerability and Growth: Embrace vulnerability as a pathway to growth and transformation, allowing yourself to be open and receptive to new insights, experiences, and challenges that deepen your understanding of yourself, others, and the divine mysteries of existence.

Lifelong Learning and Exploration: Embrace a mindset of lifelong learning and exploration, remain open to diverse perspectives, traditions, and interpretations within Christianity and beyond, and engage in dialogue and inquiry that expands your understanding and enriches your spiritual journey.

Inclusive Leadership and Community Engagement

Inclusive Leadership: Foster inclusive leadership that empowers individuals from diverse backgrounds and perspectives to contribute their gifts and talents to the community, creating opportunities for shared leadership, collaboration, and collective decision-making that reflect the richness and diversity of the body of Christ.

Community Engagement: Engage with the broader community in meaningful and transformative ways, partnering with other faith-based organizations, nonprofit agencies, and community groups to address pressing social issues, serve those in need, and build bridges of understanding and solidarity across divides.

In summary, the vision for a more compassionate and authentic expression of Christianity calls for a faith community that embodies the values and teachings of Jesus Christ in tangible ways, fostering a culture of compassion, inclusivity, and genuine spiritual growth. By embracing this vision, individuals and communities can contribute to realizing God's kingdom on earth, where love, justice, and mercy abound, and all are welcomed and affirmed as beloved children of God.

Examples Of Doing The Devil's Work Behind The Christian Maks

Examples of doing the devil's work behind the Christian mask involve using religious language, symbols, or authority to justify or conceal immoral behavior, thereby distorting the true essence of Christianity and causing harm to oneself and others.

These examples illustrate how individuals may distort or misuse religious beliefs and practices for selfish, divisive, or harmful purposes, undermining the principles of love, compassion, and integrity that lie at the heart of authentic Christianity. It is incumbent upon Christians to remain vigilant and discerning, actively challenging and confronting such behaviors and striving to embody the true spirit of Christ in all aspects of their lives and interactions.

People Doing The Devil's Work

When people engage in actions contrary to the core principles of Christianity while professing to be devout followers, it can be described as doing the devil's work behind the Christian mask. This concept highlights the dissonance between outward appearances and inner motivations, where individuals use their Christian identity as a facade to conceal their true intentions or actions.

One example of doing the devil's work behind the Christian mask is when individuals exploit their positions of power or authority within religious institutions for personal gain or to manipulate others. This could involve financial misconduct, such as embezzlement or fraud, where individuals misuse funds meant for charitable purposes for their enrichment. Similarly, leaders might abuse their authority to engage in inappropriate or abusive behavior, betraying the trust of their followers and causing harm to those under their care.

Another manifestation of this phenomenon is when individuals use religious rhetoric to justify discriminatory or harmful actions toward others. This could take the form of spreading hateful or divisive messages under the guise of spiritual teachings, fostering bigotry or intolerance towards marginalized groups such as LGBTQ+ individuals, immigrants, or people of different faiths. By cloaking their prejudices in religious language, these individuals deceive others into believing that their actions are morally justified when, in reality, they are perpetuating harm and injustice.

Furthermore, some people may engage in hypocritical behavior, publicly espousing Christian values such as love, forgiveness, and humility while privately harboring resentment, grudges, or a judgmental attitude toward others. This discrepancy between professed beliefs and actual behavior undermines the credibility of their Christian witness. It contributes to a sense of disillusionment and mistrust within religious communities.

Overall, when individuals use their Christian identity as a mask to conceal behaviors that contradict the teachings of Christ, they are engaging in the devil's work behind the Christian mask. This behavior not only tarnishes the reputation of Christianity but also causes harm to others and perpetuates hypocrisy and moral inconsistency within religious communities.

Examples

Abuse of Spiritual Authority: Certain religious leaders or figures may abuse their spiritual authority to manipulate or control others, using fear tactics or threats of divine punishment to maintain power over their followers. This exploitation of trust and vulnerability can have devastating consequences for those affected.

Censorship and Suppression of Dissent: In some religious communities, there may be a culture of censorship and suppression of dissenting voices or alternative perspectives. This stifling of open dialogue and critical inquiry can lead to stagnation and dogmatism within the community, hindering intellectual and spiritual growth.

Censorship and Suppression of Dissenting Theological Views: Within academic or theological circles, censorship or suppression of dissenting views may challenge orthodox interpretations of Christian doctrine. This stifling of intellectual inquiry can inhibit theological diversity and hinder the growth and development of Christian thought.

Church Leaders Engaged in Power Struggles: Power struggles and conflicts can arise among clergy or leadership figures within religious institutions. Instead of prioritizing their congregation's or community's well-being, some leaders may focus on consolidating their power or advancing their personal agendas, leading to division and discord within the faith community.

Church Leaders Involved in Abuse Cover-Ups: In various denominations, there have been cases where church leaders, including pastors, priests, and bishops, have been implicated in covering up instances of sexual abuse within their congregations or institutions. These cover-ups not only betrayed the trust of victims and their families but also undermined the integrity of the Christian community.

Commercialization of Christian Holidays: In modern consumer culture, Christian holidays such as Christmas and Easter have become highly commercialized, emphasizing consumerism and materialism rather than spiritual reflection and observance. This commercialization can detract from the true meaning of these holidays and undermine their religious significance.

Commercialization of Spiritual Practices: Some individuals or organizations may commercialize spiritual practices, such as meditation, mindfulness, or yoga, by packaging them as Christian products or services without regard for their cultural or religious origins. This commodification can dilute the spiritual significance of these practices and promote a superficial understanding of spirituality.

Cultural Appropriation in Worship Practices: In multicultural contexts, there may be cultural appropriation within Christian worship practices, where elements of non-Christian cultures are adopted without proper understanding or respect for their origins and significance. This appropriation can disrespect the cultural heritage of marginalized communities and reinforce power imbalances.

Cultural Appropriation of Christian Symbols for Non-Christian Purposes: In some cases, Christian symbols or rituals may be appropriated for non-religious or commercial purposes, stripping them of their sacred significance and turning them into commodities. This can dilute the spiritual meaning of these symbols and contribute to a superficial understanding of Christianity.

Cultural Hegemony in Christian Missionary Work: In missionary efforts, there may be a tendency to impose Western cultural values or norms alongside Christian teachings, eroding indigenous cultures and traditions. This cultural hegemony can undermine the autonomy and dignity of local communities and hinder genuine engagement with Christianity on their terms.

Cultural Imperialism in Missionary Work: In some cases, missionary efforts by Christian organizations or individuals may be motivated by a desire to impose Western cultural values or norms on indigenous peoples or communities rather than genuinely seeking to share the message of Christianity in a respectful and culturally sensitive manner.

Cultural Stereotyping and Otherization: In missionary efforts or cross-cultural interactions, Christians may perpetuate cultural stereotypes or engage in otherization, viewing non-Christian cultures as primitive or inferior and imposing Western values or norms onto them. This ethnocentrism can hinder genuine dialogue and mutual understanding between cultural and religious communities.

Cultural Stereotyping in Evangelistic Efforts: In evangelistic efforts, there may be a tendency to stereotype or caricature non-Christian cultures or beliefs, portraying them as primitive or backward compared to Christianity. This cultural insensitivity can hinder genuine dialogue and understanding between different cultural and religious communities.

Discrimination and Prejudice: Some individuals and groups have used Christianity as a justification for bigotry and prejudice against marginalized communities, including LGBTQ+ individuals, immigrants, and religious minorities. By invoking religious teachings out of context or selectively interpreting scripture, they perpetuate harmful stereotypes and contribute to social divisions.

Divisive Interpretations of End-Times Prophecy: Interpretations of end-times prophecy in Christian theology can sometimes lead to divisive beliefs and attitudes, fostering an "us-versus-them" mentality towards those perceived as outsiders or enemies. This divisiveness can hinder efforts towards peace, cooperation, and understanding.

Exaggerated Claims of Miraculous Healing: Some individuals or groups within Christian circles may make exaggerated claims about miraculous healings or interventions, exploiting the hopes and vulnerabilities of those seeking spiritual or physical relief. This manipulation can lead to disillusionment and skepticism within the broader community.

Exploitation of Religious Authority for Political Gain: Some political leaders may exploit their religious authority or affiliation for political gain, using religious rhetoric or symbolism to appeal to religious voters without genuine commitment to Christian values or principles. This exploitation can manipulate public sentiment and undermine the integrity of both religion and politics.

Exploitation of Religious Authority in Corporate Culture: Some corporations may exploit religious authority or symbolism in their corporate culture, using religious language or rituals to foster a sense of community or loyalty among employees without genuine commitment to ethical or moral principles. This exploitation can manipulate employees' faith and values for corporate interests.

Exploitation of Religious Authority in Family Dynamics: Within families, individuals in positions of religious authority, such as parents or elders, may exploit their status to enforce strict religious norms or control the behavior of other family members. This exploitation can lead to conflicts between individual autonomy and religious conformity, causing harm to familial relationships and personal development.

Exploitation of Religious Beliefs for Financial Gain: Some individuals or organizations may exploit the religious beliefs of vulnerable individuals for financial gain, such as through the sale of overpriced religious merchandise, bogus miracle cures, or fraudulent religious investments. This exploitation can prey on the trust and faith of believers, leading to financial loss and disillusionment.

Exploitation of Religious Fear and Guilt: Some religious leaders or organizations may use fear-based tactics or guilt-tripping to manipulate individuals into compliance or adherence to certain beliefs or practices. This exploitation of religious fear and guilt can lead to psychological harm and emotional manipulation among followers.

Exploitation of Religious Fears for Control: Some religious leaders or organizations may exploit fears of divine punishment or spiritual consequences to control or manipulate their followers, instilling a sense of guilt or shame to maintain obedience and loyalty. This exploitation of religious fears can lead to psychological harm and spiritual abuse among believers.

DOING THE DEVIL'S WORK BEHIND THE CHRISTIAN MASK

Exploitation of Religious Fervor for Political Gain: In some instances, politicians and political parties have exploited religious fervor among specific population segments to advance their political agendas. They may use religious language and symbolism to appeal to voters, even if their policies or actions do not align with Christian values of compassion, justice, and integrity.

Exploitation of Religious Guilt for Recruitment: Cults or extremist groups may exploit feelings of guilt or unworthiness in individuals, promising salvation or redemption through membership in their group or adherence to their beliefs. This manipulation can lead vulnerable individuals into abusive or coercive relationships under the guise of religious devotion.

Exploitation of Religious Hospitality: Christian hospitality, which emphasizes welcoming strangers and caring for the marginalized, may be exploited by individuals or organizations for personal gain or ulterior motives. This exploitation can betray the trust of those in need and tarnish the reputation of genuine acts of kindness and hospitality.

Exploitation of Religious Identity for Economic Gain: Some businesses or entrepreneurs may exploit Christian identity or themes for economic gain, marketing products or services using religious symbols or language without genuine adherence to Christian values. This commercialization can trivialize sacred beliefs and practices and erode the spiritual integrity of the Christian faith.

Exploitation of Religious Identity for Marketing Purposes: Some businesses or organizations may exploit religious identity or affiliation for marketing purposes, using religious symbolism or language to appeal to consumers' sense of identity or values. This exploitation can trivialize sacred beliefs and practices and commodify spirituality for commercial gain.

Exploitation of Religious Identity for Political Opportunism: Politicians or public figures may exploit their religious identity or affiliation for political opportunism, using religious rhetoric or symbolism to appeal to specific voter demographics without genuine commitment to Christian principles or values. This exploitation can erode public trust and integrity in the political process.

Exploitation of Religious Identity in Advertising: Advertisers may exploit religious identity in marketing campaigns, using religious themes or symbols to appeal to consumers' emotions or values and enhance brand recognition without genuine respect for religious beliefs or practices. This exploitation can trivialize sacred traditions and offend individuals' religious sensibilities.

Exploitation of Religious Identity in Corporate Branding: Corporations may exploit religious identity in their branding strategies. They use religious symbolism or language to appeal to consumers' values or emotions and enhance their marketability without a genuine commitment to ethical or moral principles. This exploitation can trivialize sacred beliefs and practices and commercialize spirituality for profit.

Exploitation of Religious Identity in Cultural Appropriation: Non-Christian individuals or groups may exploit Christian religious identity in cultural appropriation, appropriating religious symbols, practices, or imagery for commercial or artistic purposes without genuine understanding or respect for their sacred significance. This exploitation can perpetuate stereotypes and disrespect religious beliefs and traditions.

The Exploitation of Religious Identity in Disaster Relief Efforts: Some humanitarian organizations may exploit their religious identity in disaster relief efforts, using it as a marketing tool to solicit donations or gain public support without a genuine commitment to adequate and equitable humanitarian assistance. This exploitation can undermine trust in charitable organizations and hinder relief efforts for affected communities.

Exploitation of Religious Identity in Interfaith Dialogue: Some individuals or organizations may exploit their religious identity in interfaith dialogue, using it to assert dominance or superiority over other faith traditions rather than fostering genuine understanding, respect, and cooperation. This exploitation can hinder efforts towards religious harmony and peacebuilding.

Exploitation of Religious Identity in Media Representations: Media representations of religious identity may be exploited for sensationalism or stereotypes, perpetuating misconceptions or prejudices about religious groups and individuals. This exploitation can contribute to the stigmatization of religious minorities and reinforce social divisions and tensions.

Exploitation of Religious Identity in Online Spaces: Online platforms may exploit religious identity for targeted advertising or content delivery, using algorithms to categorize individuals based on their perceived religious affiliations and preferences. This exploitation can invade individuals' privacy and contribute to the polarization of online communities.

DOING THE DEVIL'S WORK BEHIND THE CHRISTIAN MASK

Exploitation of Religious Identity in Political Campaigns: Political candidates or parties may exploit religious identity in election campaigns, using religious rhetoric or symbolism to appeal to voters' values or beliefs and gain electoral support without genuine commitment to Christian principles or ethical governance. This exploitation can manipulate public sentiment and undermine the integrity of democratic processes.

Exploitation of Religious Identity in the Tourism Industry: The tourism industry may exploit religious identity for commercial gain, promoting religious sites or pilgrimage destinations as tourist attractions without regard for their sacred significance or impact on local communities. This exploitation can commodify spirituality and trivialize religious beliefs and practices.

Exploitation of Religious Identity in Tourism Marketing: Tourism marketers may exploit religious identity in destination marketing, promoting religious sites or pilgrimage routes as tourist attractions to attract visitors and generate revenue without genuinely considering these sites' cultural and spiritual significance. This exploitation can lead to overcrowding, commercialization, and cultural commodification.

Exploitation of Religious Rituals for Tourism: Religious rituals or ceremonies may be exploited for tourism purposes, with sacred sites or practices commodified for the entertainment or curiosity of tourists. This exploitation can disrespect sacred traditions and trivialize the spiritual significance of religious rituals and artifacts.

Exploitation of Religious Symbols for Commercial Gain: In the marketplace, religious symbols and iconography may be exploited for commercial gain, with little regard for their sacred significance. This commercialization of religious imagery can trivialize the spiritual meaning behind these symbols and contribute to a culture of consumerism.

Exploitation of Religious Symbols for Commercialization: Some businesses or advertisers may exploit religious symbols or imagery for commercial purposes, using religious holidays or themes to promote consumer products or services. This exploitation can trivialize sacred beliefs and practices and erode the spiritual significance of religious symbols in the public sphere.

Exploitation of Religious Symbols for Political Power: Political leaders or groups may co-opt religious symbols or language to consolidate power or mobilize support for their agendas. This instrumentalization of religion for political gain can lead to the manipulation of religious beliefs and sentiments for secular ends.

Exploitation of Religious Symbols in the Fashion Industry: The fashion industry may exploit religious symbols or imagery for commercial purposes, using religious iconography in clothing or accessories without regard for their sacred significance. This exploitation can trivialize religious beliefs and practices and offend individuals of faith.

Exploitation of Religious Symbols in Political Propaganda: Political parties or movements may exploit Christian religious symbols or imagery for political propaganda, manipulating public sentiment or rallying support for particular agendas without genuine commitment to Christian values or principles. This exploitation can distort the true meaning of religious symbols and undermine their sacred significance.

Exploitation of Religious Symbols in Pop Culture: Pop culture may exploit religious symbols or imagery for shock value or entertainment, using religious themes in music, film, or art without genuine reverence or respect for their sacred significance. This exploitation can trivialize religious beliefs and practices and contribute to cultural misunderstandings.

Exploitation of Religious Titles for Personal Gain: Some individuals may exploit religious titles or positions, such as pastor or spiritual leader, for personal gain or influence, using their perceived authority to manipulate or exploit others for financial or other benefits. This exploitation can damage trust within religious communities and tarnish the reputation of genuine spiritual leaders.

Exploitation of Religious Trust in Charitable Organizations: Charitable organizations or NGOs may exploit religious trust to solicit donations or support for their causes, using religious language or imagery to appeal to donors' sense of moral obligation or spiritual duty. This exploitation can divert resources from genuine charitable efforts and undermine public trust in philanthropy.

Exploitation of Religious Trust in Financial Schemes: Scammers or fraudsters may exploit religious trust and community networks to perpetrate financial schemes or Ponzi schemes, targeting individuals more likely to trust those within their spiritual community. This exploitation can lead to financial loss and betrayal of trust among believers.

DOING THE DEVIL'S WORK BEHIND THE CHRISTIAN MASK

Exploitation of Religious Vulnerability in Marketing: Advertisers or marketers may exploit religious symbols or themes to manipulate consumer behavior, tapping into the emotional vulnerability of religious individuals to sell products or services. This exploitation can trivialize sacred beliefs and cheapen the spiritual significance of religious symbols.

Exploitative Religious Cults: Some groups may form around charismatic leaders who claim divine authority and manipulate followers through psychological, emotional, or physical coercion. These cults often isolate members from outside influences, imbuing them with distorted interpretations of Christian teachings and exploiting their devotion for the leader's personal gain.

Failure to Address Systemic Injustices: Some Christian communities may fail to address systemic injustices such as racism, sexism, or economic inequality within their ranks, prioritizing individual salvation over collective liberation. This neglect of social responsibility undermines the transformative potential of Christianity to challenge and change oppressive structures.

False Prophets Exploiting Vulnerable Followers: Throughout history, individuals have claimed to have unique insight or communication with God, leading followers to believe in their divine authority. These false prophets often manipulate vulnerable followers for personal gain, whether financially, emotionally, or physically.

Hypocritical Public Figures: There have been instances of public figures who publicly espouse Christian values but engage in behavior that contradicts those values in private. This could include cases of infidelity, dishonesty, or unethical conduct. While their public personas may project piety and morality, their private actions reveal a different reality.

Manipulation of Religious Symbols for Political Propaganda: Political leaders or parties may manipulate religious symbols or rituals for propaganda, using religious imagery to rally support or demonize opponents. This manipulation can distort the true meaning of religious symbols and undermine the integrity of religious beliefs and practices.

Manipulation of Religious Texts for Political Ideology: Political leaders or groups may manipulate religious texts or teachings to support their political ideology or agenda, cherry-picking passages that align with their views while ignoring broader principles of love, compassion, and justice. This distortion of religious scripture can mislead followers and contribute to societal polarization and division.

Misrepresentation of Christian History in Education: In educational settings, there may be a tendency to whitewash or sanitize Christian history, glossing over instances of violence, oppression, or intolerance perpetrated by Christians or Christian institutions. This distortion of history can perpetuate myths and stereotypes, hindering critical understanding and reflection.

Misrepresentation of Christian Values in Media: In popular culture, portrayals of Christians and Christianity may reinforce stereotypes or misconceptions that do not accurately reflect the diversity and complexity of Christian beliefs and practices. This misrepresentation can perpetuate misunderstandings and prejudice towards Christians in broader society.

Misuse of Religious Authority for Personal Gain: Religious leaders or figures may abuse their authority within religious communities to control their followers or enrich themselves financially. They may manipulate or coerce their followers into making financial contributions, providing free labor, or engaging in other forms of exploitation under the guise of religious duty.

Misuse of Religious Authority for Personal Vendettas: In hierarchical religious structures, individuals in positions of authority may abuse their power to settle personal scores or pursue vendettas against perceived enemies within their community. This misuse of religious authority can lead to manipulation, coercion, and spiritual abuse of vulnerable individuals.

Misuse of Religious Language for Emotional Manipulation: Some individuals or groups may use religious language or rhetoric to emotionally manipulate others, invoking themes of sin, salvation, and divine judgment to induce feelings of guilt, shame, or fear. This emotional manipulation can lead to psychological harm and spiritual distress among vulnerable individuals.

Misuse of Religious Language in Marketing Campaigns: Marketing campaigns may misuse religious language or imagery to evoke emotions or manipulate consumer behavior, using religious themes to sell products or services without genuine reverence or respect for their sacred significance. This misuse can trivialize religious beliefs and practices and exploit consumers' spiritual sensibilities.

Misuse of Religious Language in Political Rhetoric: Politicians or public figures may misuse religious language or rhetoric to appeal to religious voters or justify their political agenda, invoking divine authority to sanctify their policies or actions. This manipulation can lead to the politicization of religion and undermine the separation of church and state.

Misuse of Religious Platforms for Personal Promotion: Some individuals may misuse religious platforms, such as churches or religious organizations, for personal promotion or self-aggrandizement, using their positions to gain influence, status, or financial gain. This misuse can undermine the integrity and credibility of religious institutions and harm the trust of congregants or followers.

Misuse of Religious Rituals for Superstition or Magical Thinking: Some individuals may engage in religious rituals or practices for superstitious or magical purposes, seeking to manipulate divine forces for personal gain or protection. This misuse of religious rituals can lead to a shallow understanding of spirituality and diminish the transformative power of genuine faith.

Misuse of Religious Symbols for Cultural Appropriation: Non-Christian individuals or groups may appropriate Christian symbols or imagery for cultural or artistic purposes without understanding or respecting their religious significance. This cultural appropriation can trivialize sacred beliefs and practices and contribute to misunderstanding and disrespect toward Christian communities.

Misuse of Spiritual Gifts for Personal Gain: Individuals within Christian communities may claim to possess spiritual gifts, such as prophecy or healing, and use these claims to gain influence or financial support. This exploitation of spiritual beliefs and practices for personal profit undermines the authenticity of genuine spiritual experiences and fosters skepticism within the broader community.

Neglect of Social Justice in Favor of Personal Prosperity: In prosperity gospel teachings, individuals may prioritize personal wealth and success as signs of divine favor while neglecting the call to address systemic injustices and societal inequalities. This distortion of Christian teachings can perpetuate a self-centered and materialistic worldview that contradicts the values of humility, compassion, and service.

Political Leaders Using Religion for Manipulation: Throughout history, political leaders have often invoked religious rhetoric to justify wars, conquests, and acts of oppression. For example, during the Crusades, European rulers used

Christian ideology to justify military campaigns against Muslim territories in the Holy Land. Similarly, in modern times, some politicians have exploited Christian beliefs to garner support for discriminatory policies or nationalist agendas.

Political Manipulation of Religious Institutions: Political leaders or organizations may seek to co-opt religious institutions for their political agendas, using religion to mobilize voters or justify government policies. This manipulation of religious sentiment for political gain undermines the autonomy of religious communities and compromises their spiritual integrity.

Religious Discrimination in Access to Education Resources: Individuals may face religious discrimination when accessing educational resources, such as being denied funding or support for religiously affiliated schools or programs based on institutional bias or government regulations. This discrimination can limit educational opportunities and hinder academic freedom and diversity.

Religious Discrimination in Access to Education Resources: Individuals may face religious discrimination when accessing educational resources, such as being denied funding or support for religiously affiliated schools or programs based on institutional bias or government regulations. This discrimination can limit educational opportunities and hinder academic freedom and diversity.

Religious Discrimination in Access to Education: Some individuals may face religious discrimination when seeking access to education, such as being denied enrollment or facing harassment or exclusion from educational opportunities due to their religious beliefs or practices. This discrimination can limit individuals' opportunities for personal growth and development.

Religious Discrimination in Access to Employment Opportunities: Some individuals may face religious discrimination when seeking employment, such as being denied job opportunities or harassment or discrimination in the workplace based on their religious beliefs or practices. This discrimination can limit individuals' career prospects and hinder economic mobility.

Religious Discrimination in Access to Financial Resources: Some individuals or communities may face religious discrimination when accessing financial resources, such as being denied loans or investment opportunities based on their religious beliefs or affiliations. This discrimination can hinder economic development and perpetuate financial exclusion and poverty.

DOING THE DEVIL'S WORK BEHIND THE CHRISTIAN MASK

Religious Discrimination in Access to Financial Services: Individuals may face religious discrimination when seeking financial services, such as being denied loans or banking services based on religious or cultural identifiers. This discrimination can exacerbate economic inequalities and hinder individuals' financial stability and opportunities for socioeconomic advancement.

Religious Discrimination in Access to Healthcare Services: Individuals may face religious discrimination when seeking healthcare services, such as being denied reproductive healthcare options or end-of-life care based on healthcare providers' religious objections. This discrimination can infringe upon individuals' rights to make autonomous decisions about their health and well-being.

Religious Discrimination in Access to Legal Representation: Individuals may face religious discrimination when seeking legal representation, such as being denied representation or receiving inadequate legal support due to attorney bias or prejudice based on their religious beliefs or practices. This discrimination can undermine individuals' access to justice and fair legal proceedings.

Religious Discrimination in Access to Legal Representation: Individuals may face religious discrimination when seeking legal representation, such as being denied counsel or receiving inadequate legal support due to attorney bias or prejudice based on their religious beliefs or practices. This discrimination can undermine individuals' access to justice and fair legal proceedings.

Religious Discrimination in Access to Legal Representation: Individuals may face religious discrimination when seeking legal representation, such as being denied counsel or receiving inadequate legal support due to attorney bias or prejudice based on their religious beliefs or practices. This discrimination can undermine individuals' access to justice and fair legal proceedings.

Religious Discrimination in Access to Public Services: Some individuals may face religious discrimination when accessing public services, such as being denied government benefits or assistance based on their religious beliefs or affiliations. This discrimination can exacerbate social inequalities and marginalization among already vulnerable populations.

Religious Discrimination in Access to Public Services: Some individuals may face religious discrimination when accessing public services, such as being denied government benefits or assistance based on their religious beliefs or affiliations. This discrimination can exacerbate social inequalities and marginalization among already vulnerable populations.

Religious Discrimination in Access to Public Services: Some individuals may face religious discrimination when accessing public services, such as being denied government benefits or assistance based on their religious beliefs or affiliations. This discrimination can exacerbate social inequalities and marginalization among already vulnerable populations.

Religious Discrimination in Access to Public Services: Some individuals may face religious discrimination when accessing public services, such as being denied government benefits or assistance based on their religious beliefs or affiliations. This discrimination can exacerbate social inequalities and marginalization among already vulnerable populations.

Religious Discrimination in Access to Social Services: Some individuals may face religious discrimination when seeking access to social services, such as being denied assistance or support based on their religious beliefs or affiliations. This discrimination can exacerbate vulnerabilities and marginalization among already disadvantaged populations.

Religious Discrimination in Access to Social Services: Some individuals or communities may face religious discrimination when accessing social services, such as being denied government assistance or support based on their religious beliefs or affiliations. This discrimination can exacerbate social inequalities and perpetuate cycles of poverty and marginalization.

Religious Discrimination in Access to Social Services: Some individuals or communities may face religious discrimination when accessing social services, such as being denied government assistance or support based on their religious beliefs or affiliations. This discrimination can exacerbate social inequalities and perpetuate cycles of poverty and marginalization.

Religious Discrimination in Access to Social Services: Some individuals or communities may face religious discrimination when accessing social services, such as being denied government assistance or support based on their religious beliefs or affiliations. This discrimination can exacerbate social inequalities and perpetuate cycles of poverty and marginalization.

Religious Discrimination in Access to Social Services: Some individuals or communities may face religious discrimination when accessing social services, such as being denied government assistance or support based on their religious beliefs or affiliations. This discrimination can exacerbate social inequalities and perpetuate cycles of poverty and marginalization.

Religious Discrimination in Adoption and Foster Care Services: Some adoption and foster care agencies may discriminate against individuals or couples based on their religious beliefs or practices, such as refusing to place children with LGBTQ+ individuals or couples due to religious objections. This discrimination can limit options for children needing stable and loving homes.

Religious Discrimination in Education: In educational settings, individuals may face religious discrimination or bias from peers or educators, such as ridicule or ostracization for their religious beliefs or practices. This discrimination can create hostile environments and hinder students' ability to learn and grow in a diverse and inclusive community.

Religious Discrimination in Employment: In some workplaces or industries, individuals may face religious discrimination or harassment based on their beliefs or practices, such as being denied employment opportunities or promotions due to their religious affiliation. This discrimination can violate individuals' rights to religious freedom and equal treatment under the law.

Religious Discrimination in Healthcare Access: Some individuals may face religious discrimination when seeking healthcare services, such as being denied access to specific medical treatments or procedures due to objections by healthcare providers based on their religious beliefs. This discrimination can compromise individuals' health and well-being and violate their rights to medical care.

Religious Discrimination in Healthcare: In healthcare settings, individuals may face religious discrimination or denial of services based on their beliefs or practices, such as being denied access to reproductive healthcare or end-of-life options due to religious objections by healthcare providers. This discrimination can violate individuals' rights to autonomy and dignity in medical decision-making.

Religious Discrimination in Housing Policies: Some individuals may face religious discrimination in housing policies or practices, such as being denied housing opportunities or facing harassment or eviction based on their religious beliefs or practices. This discrimination can infringe upon individuals' rights to safe and stable housing and contribute to social exclusion.

Religious Discrimination in Housing: In housing markets, individuals may face religious discrimination or bias when seeking housing accommodations, such as being denied rental or purchase opportunities due to their religious beliefs or practices. This discrimination can limit individuals' access to housing and perpetuate social inequalities.

Religious Discrimination in Legal Proceedings: In legal proceedings, individuals may face religious discrimination or bias from judges, lawyers, or jurors, such as being mistreated or receiving harsher penalties due to their religious beliefs or practices. This discrimination can undermine the principles of justice and equality under the law.

Religious Discrimination in Legal Representation: In legal proceedings, individuals may face religious discrimination when seeking legal representation, such as being denied counsel or receiving inadequate representation due to attorney bias or prejudice based on their religious beliefs or practices. This discrimination can undermine individuals' access to justice and fair legal proceedings.

Religious Discrimination in Legal Systems: Individuals may face religious discrimination or bias based on their beliefs or practices, such as being subject to harsher penalties or unfair treatment due to religious prejudice by judges or juries. This discrimination can undermine the principles of justice and equality under the law.

Religious Discrimination in Workplace Accommodations: Some individuals may face religious discrimination in the workplace, such as being denied reasonable accommodations for religious practices or observances due to employer bias or ignorance. This discrimination can infringe upon individuals' rights to religious freedom and equal treatment in employment.

Religious Elitism and Spiritual Pride: Some individuals or groups within Christian communities may develop a sense of spiritual superiority, looking d upon those they perceive as less devout or less spiritually enlightened. This elitism can lead to arrogance and judgmental attitudes towards others, contradicting the teachings of humility and love.

Religious Elitism in Spiritual Communities: Within Christian communities, there may be a tendency towards religious elitism, with specific individuals or groups asserting their spiritual superiority or exclusive access to divine revelation. This elitism can foster arrogance and exclusivity, hindering genuine fellowship and unity within the faith community.

Religious Exclusion and Marginalization: Some Christian communities may engage in practices of exclusion and marginalization, ostracizing or discriminating against individuals who do not conform to specific religious or cultural norms. This behavior contradicts the teachings of Christ, who welcomed all people regardless of their background or status.

Religious Exclusivity and Sectarianism: Some Christian denominations or sects may promote exclusivity and sectarianism, claiming to be the only true representatives of Christianity while denigrating or excluding other Christian groups. This attitude can lead to division and conflict within the broader Christian community, hindering cooperation and unity among believers.

Religious Exclusivity in Social Circles: Some Christian social circles may exhibit exclusivity, where individuals primarily associate with others who share their religious beliefs, leading to insular communities close to those outside their faith. This exclusivity can hinder meaningful interaction and understanding with people of diverse backgrounds.

Religious Exclusivity in Social Circles: Within Christian social circles, there may be tendencies towards exclusivity or cliquishness, where specific individuals or groups are marginalized or excluded based on socioeconomic status, race, or theological beliefs. This exclusivity contradicts the inclusive message of Christianity and fosters division within the faith community.

Religious Extremism and Intolerance: In extreme cases, individuals or groups may use religion as a pretext for extremism, violence, or terrorism. By distorting religious teachings to justify acts of hatred or intolerance towards others, they not only betray the principles of Christianity but also pose a threat to peace and security in society.

Religious Fundamentalism and Dogmatism: In specific Christian communities, there may be a tendency towards rigid fundamentalism and dogmatism, where strict doctrinal interpretations precede critical thinking or open dialogue. This closed-mindedness can lead to intolerance towards differing perspectives and hinder intellectual growth and spiritual maturity.

Religious Gatekeeping and Excommunication: Some Christian communities may engage in practices of gatekeeping or excommunication, excluding individuals or groups deemed heretical or disobedient to church authority. This exclusionary approach can lead to ostracism and trauma for those who do not conform to established norms or beliefs.

Religious Gatekeeping in Interfaith Dialogue: In interfaith dialogue or cooperation, some Christians may engage in religious gatekeeping, asserting their religious beliefs or practices as normative or superior to those of other faith traditions. This gatekeeping can hinder genuine dialogue and mutual respect between different religious communities.

Religious Gatekeeping in Leadership Roles: Within Christian institutions, there may be barriers to leadership roles for specific individuals based on gender, race, or sexual orientation. This religious gatekeeping can limit opportunities for diverse voices and perspectives to contribute to the leadership and direction of the church.

Religious Hypocrisy in Political Scandals: In political scandals involving Christian politicians or leaders, there may be religious hypocrisy, where individuals publicly espouse Christian values while privately engaging in behavior that contradicts those values. This hypocrisy can erode public trust in religious leaders and institutions and undermine the credibility of Christian ethics in the public sphere.

Religious Hypocrisy in Public Life: Individuals who publicly identify as Christian may engage in behavior that contradicts Christian values in their personal or professional lives. This hypocrisy can erode public trust in the Christian faith and reinforce negative stereotypes about Christians as judgmental or insincere.

Religious Idolatry of Material Wealth: In prosperity gospel teachings, material wealth and success are often equated with divine favor. This leads to a fixation on material possessions and financial prosperity as signs of spiritual blessing. This idolatry of material wealth can foster greed and materialism, distorting the valid values of Christianity.

Religious Idolatry of Political Figures: Some Christians may elevate political figures or leaders to idols, placing unwavering loyalty and trust in them as saviors or messianic figures. This idolatry can lead to the uncritical acceptance of harmful policies or actions and compromise the prophetic witness of the Christian community.

Religious Intolerance and Discrimination: Despite Christianity's teachings of love and acceptance, some individuals or groups may use their faith as justification for discrimination or violence against those who hold different beliefs or identities. This bigotry and intolerance contradict the inclusive message of Christianity and contribute to division and hatred in society.

Religious Intolerance in Interfaith Relations: Christians may engage in religious intolerance or exclusivism in their interactions with individuals of other faiths, viewing non-Christian beliefs as inferior or misguided. This attitude can hinder dialogue and cooperation between religious communities and perpetuate interfaith tensions.

Religious Justification of Authoritarianism: Some authoritarian regimes or leaders may co-opt religious rhetoric or symbols to legitimize their authority and suppress dissent or opposition. This misuse of religion can lead to the suppression of religious freedom and human rights, as well as the manipulation of religious sentiment for political ends.

Religious Justification of Economic Exploitation: Economic exploitation or injustice may be justified or rationalized through religious narratives of divine providence or reward, leading to the neglect or exploitation of vulnerable populations in pursuit of profit or economic growth. This exploitation can perpetuate cycles of poverty and inequality, undermining the principles of social justice and solidarity.

Religious Justification of Environmental Exploitation: Despite Christianity's call for stewardship of the earth, some individuals or industries may justify environmental exploitation or destruction through religious narratives of dominion or divine providence. This exploitation can contribute to ecological degradation and disregard for the interconnectedness of all creation.

Religious Justification of Militarism or Nationalism: Some Christians may use religious language or imagery to justify militaristic or nationalistic agendas, glorifying violence or aggression as a means of defending or advancing their perceived religious or political interests. This conflation of religion with patriotism can lead to dangerous forms of religious extremism and conflict.

Religious Justification of Social Hierarchies: Some Christians may use religious teachings to justify social hierarchies or inequalities, promoting patriarchal or hierarchical interpretations of scripture that privilege certain groups or individuals over others. This justification of social hierarchies can perpetuate discrimination and marginalization based on gender, race, or socioeconomic status.

Religious Persecution of Dissenters: Throughout history, some Christians have persecuted or ostracized fellow believers who held dissenting views or challenged established religious authorities. This suppression of dissent stifles intellectual and spiritual growth within the Christian community. It perpetuates a culture of fear and conformity.

Religious Polarization in Political Discourse: In political discourse, there may be a tendency to polarize issues along religious lines, with Christians divided into opposing camps based on partisan or ideological affiliations. This polarization can hinder constructive dialogue and cooperation on matters of common concern and reinforce divisions within the Christian community.

Religious Segregation in Communities: Some Christian communities may be characterized by religious segregation, with individuals or groups isolating themselves from those who do not share their beliefs or practices. This segregation can foster insularity and intolerance towards outsiders and hinder interfaith dialogue and cooperation opportunities.

Religious Segregation in Education: In educational settings, there may be a tendency towards religious segregation, with students from different religious backgrounds attending separate schools or receiving separate religious instruction. This segregation can reinforce religious divisions and hinder opportunities for interfaith dialogue and understanding.

Religious Segregation in Social Networks: Within social networks or online communities, individuals may self-segregate along religious lines, surrounding themselves with like-minded individuals and excluding those who do not share their religious beliefs or worldview. This segregation can lead to echo chambers and reinforce ideological polarization, hindering constructive dialogue and understanding opportunities.

Religious Supremacy and Colonialism: Throughout history, Christianity has been used to justify colonialism, imperialism, and the subjugation of indigenous peoples under the guise of spreading the gospel. This legacy of religious supremacy has left lasting scars on marginalized communities and perpetuated systems of oppression and inequality.

Religious Tribalism and Sectarianism: Some Christians may adopt a tribalistic mentality, viewing members of their denomination or sect as superior to those outside their religious group. This sectarianism can foster division and hostility within the broader Christian community and hinder efforts toward unity and cooperation.

Selective Application of Biblical Law: Some individuals or groups may selectively apply specific Old Testament laws or passages while ignoring others, leading to inconsistencies and contradictions in their ethical or moral beliefs. This cherry-picking of scripture can result in legalism or moral relativism rather than a coherent ethical framework based on Christian principles.

Selective Application of Christian Charity in Foreign Aid: Some countries or organizations may selectively apply Christian charity in their foreign aid initiatives, assisting countries or regions deemed strategically or politically important while neglecting others in dire need of humanitarian support. This selective approach can perpetuate inequalities and exacerbate poverty and suffering in marginalized communities.

Selective Application of Christian Charity: In charitable endeavors, some Christians may selectively choose whom to help based on religious affiliation or adherence to specific moral standards rather than assisting all those in need regardless of their background or beliefs. This selective charity can perpetuate biases and contribute to social divisions.

Selective Application of Christian Compassion in Criminal Justice: Criminal justice systems may selectively apply Christian principles of compassion and forgiveness to certain offenders or crimes while disregarding others, leading to disparities in sentencing and rehabilitation efforts. This selective application can perpetuate cycles of punishment and marginalization and hinder opportunities for redemption and restoration.

Selective Application of Christian Compassion in Immigration Policies: Some nations or governments may claim to be Christian nations or uphold Christian values while implementing restrictive immigration policies that disregard the plight of refugees and migrants. This selective application of Christian compassion can contradict the biblical imperative to welcome the stranger and care for the marginalized.

Selective Application of Christian Ethics in Business Practices: Some Christian businesses or organizations may claim to operate according to Christian principles but engage in unethical or exploitative business practices, such as labor exploitation or environmental degradation. This hypocrisy can tarnish the reputation of Christianity and undermine its moral authority in the public sphere.

Selective Application of Christian Ethics in Environmental Policies: Some governments or policymakers may selectively apply Christian ethics to environmental policies, prioritizing economic interests over conservation efforts or disregarding the biblical mandate to care for the earth. This selective application can lead to environmental degradation and neglect of future generations' well-being.

Selective Application of Christian Ethics in Environmental Stewardship: Some Christians may selectively apply Christian ethics to environmental issues, prioritizing human dominion over nature or economic interests over ecological conservation. This selective application can lead to environmental degradation and disregard for the biblical mandate of stewardship and care for creation.

Selective Application of Christian Ethics in Global Affairs: Some nations or international organizations may selectively invoke Christian ethics or values to justify their foreign policies or interventions while disregarding principles of peace, justice, and human dignity in their actions. This selective application can lead to hypocrisy and inconsistency in diplomatic relations and hinder efforts towards global cooperation and solidarity.

Selective Application of Christian Ethics in Military Operations: Military operations may selectively invoke Christian ethics or just war theory to justify specific actions or interventions while disregarding broader principles of peace, nonviolence, and reconciliation. This selective application can lead to moral ambiguity and ethical dilemmas in military decision-making.

Selective Application of Christian Ethics in Technology Development: Technology companies may selectively apply Christian ethics in their development and deployment of new technologies, prioritizing profit and innovation over ethical considerations such as privacy, security, and social impact. This selective application can lead to the exploitation of vulnerable populations and exacerbate societal inequalities.

Selective Application of Christian Forgiveness: Christians may selectively apply the principle of forgiveness, offering forgiveness to some individuals while withholding it from others based on personal biases or judgments. This selective forgiveness can perpetuate resentment and hinder reconciliation and healing in relationships and communities.

DOING THE DEVIL'S WORK BEHIND THE CHRISTIAN MASK

Selective Application of Christian Hospitality: Christians may selectively extend hospitality to specific individuals or groups based on their perceived alignment with Christian values or beliefs while excluding or marginalizing others. This selective hospitality can perpetuate biases and hinder genuine fellowship and community building.

Selective Application of Christian Morality in Corporate Governance: Corporations may selectively apply Christian morality in their corporate governance practices, prioritizing profit and shareholder value over ethical considerations or social responsibility. This selective application can lead to exploitative labor practices, environmental degradation, and disregard for human rights.

Selective Application of Christian Morality in Criminal Justice: Criminal justice systems may selectively apply Christian morality, prioritizing punitive measures over principles of restorative justice, redemption, and rehabilitation. This selective application can perpetuate cycles of violence and retribution and hinder opportunities for reconciliation and healing in communities affected by crime.

Selective Application of Christian Morality in Criminal Prosecutions: Prosecutors may selectively apply Christian morality in criminal prosecutions, pursuing charges or seeking harsher penalties for offenses perceived as morally reprehensible while neglecting systemic injustices or addressing root causes of crime. This selective application can perpetuate disparities in the criminal justice system and hinder efforts towards restorative justice.

Selective Application of Christian Morality in Foreign Aid: Some governments or international organizations may selectively apply Christian morality to foreign aid programs, prioritizing aid to certain countries or populations perceived as morally deserving while neglecting others in need. This selective application can perpetuate inequalities and hinder efforts to address global poverty and suffering.

Selective Application of Christian Morality in Global Trade: Some nations or corporations may selectively apply Christian morality in their global trade practices, exploiting labor forces in developing countries or engaging in environmental degradation for economic gain while disregarding principles of justice, fairness, and sustainability. This selective application can perpetuate exploitation and exacerbate inequalities in the global economy.

Selective Application of Christian Morality in Healthcare Policies: Healthcare policymakers may selectively apply Christian morality in healthcare policies, prioritizing specific medical treatments or interventions based on religious beliefs or moral values while disregarding patients' rights to autonomy, dignity, and informed consent. This selective application can infringe upon individuals' healthcare rights and compromise medical ethics and standards of care.

Selective Application of Christian Morality in Healthcare Policies: Healthcare policymakers may selectively apply Christian morality in healthcare policies, prioritizing specific medical treatments or interventions based on religious beliefs or moral values while disregarding patients' rights to autonomy, dignity, and informed consent. This selective application can infringe upon individuals' healthcare rights and compromise medical ethics and standards of care.

Selective Application of Christian Morality in International Relations: Some governments or international organizations may selectively apply Christian morality in their international relations, prioritizing strategic interests or geopolitical considerations over principles of peace, justice, and human rights. This selective application can lead to conflicts, injustices, and human rights abuses worldwide.

Selective Application of Christian Morality in Media Content: Media content may selectively apply Christian morality, depicting certain behaviors or lifestyles as morally acceptable while condemning others based on subjective interpretations of religious teachings. This selective application can perpetuate stereotypes and reinforce societal divisions.

Selective Application of Christian Morality in Public Policy: Politicians or policymakers may selectively invoke Christian morality to justify specific laws or policies while ignoring others, prioritizing issues such as abortion or marriage equality over broader principles of social justice, equity, and human rights. This selective application of Christian values can perpetuate systemic inequalities and undermine the common good.

Selective Application of Christian Morality: Some individuals or groups may espouse Christian morality in certain areas while ignoring or excusing immoral behavior in others. For example, they may condemn specific social issues such as abortion or LGBTQ+ rights while turning a blind eye to systemic injustices or economic inequalities that contradict Christian principles of justice and compassion.

Selective Application of Christian Principles in Legal Interpretation: Legal scholars and practitioners may selectively interpret Christian principles in legal arguments or judgments, prioritizing certain religious beliefs or moral values over others to justify legal decisions. This selective interpretation can lead to inconsistencies in legal reasoning and undermine the impartiality and integrity of the legal system.

Selective Application of Christian Principles in Legal Interpretation: Legal scholars and practitioners may selectively interpret Christian principles in legal arguments or judgments, prioritizing certain religious beliefs or moral values over others to justify legal decisions. This selective interpretation can lead to inconsistencies in legal reasoning and undermine the impartiality and integrity of the legal system.

Selective Application of Christian Principles in Legal Interpretation: Legal scholars and practitioners may selectively interpret Christian principles in legal arguments or judgments, prioritizing certain religious beliefs or moral values over others to justify legal decisions. This selective interpretation can lead to inconsistencies in legal reasoning and undermine the impartiality and integrity of the legal system.

Selective Application of Christian Principles in Legal Interpretation: Legal scholars and practitioners may selectively interpret Christian principles in legal arguments or judgments, prioritizing certain religious beliefs or moral values over others to justify legal decisions. This selective interpretation can lead to inconsistencies in legal reasoning and undermine the impartiality and integrity of the legal system.

Selective Application of Christian Values in Environmental Policies: Some governments or corporations may selectively apply Christian values, such as stewardship and care for creation, in their environmental policies, prioritizing economic interests over conservation efforts or neglecting the impacts of environmental degradation on marginalized communities. This selective application can perpetuate environmental injustices and harm ecosystems and biodiversity.

Selective Application of Christian Values in Immigration Policies: Some nations or governments may selectively apply Christian values, such as compassion and hospitality, in their immigration policies, offering refuge to certain groups while excluding others based on nationality, ethnicity, or religion. This selective application can perpetuate discrimination and undermine the principles of justice and solidarity.

Selective Application of Christian Values in Immigration Policies: Some nations may selectively apply Christian values, such as compassion and hospitality, in their immigration policies, welcoming refugees or asylum seekers from certain countries while implementing restrictive measures or discriminatory practices against others. This selective application can perpetuate inequalities and exacerbate refugee crises and humanitarian challenges.

Selective Application of Christian Values in Immigration Policies: Some nations may selectively apply Christian values, such as compassion and hospitality, in their immigration policies, welcoming refugees or asylum seekers from certain countries while implementing restrictive measures or discriminatory practices against others. This selective application can perpetuate inequalities and exacerbate refugee crises and humanitarian challenges.

Selective Application of Forgiveness: Some individuals or communities may claim to offer forgiveness but withhold it from specific individuals or groups deemed unworthy. This selective application of forgiveness can perpetuate cycles of resentment and hinder reconciliation and healing.

Selective Application of Religious Authority in Personal Relationships: Some individuals may selectively invoke religious authority to justify power dynamics or inequalities within personal relationships, using scripture or religious teachings to maintain control or dominance over others. This misuse of spiritual authority can perpetuate patterns of abuse and exploitation in interpersonal dynamics.

Selective Compassion and Charity: While Christianity teaches compassion and charity towards those in need, some individuals or organizations may practice selective compassion, showing kindness only to those who share their beliefs or belong to their religious community. This exclusionary approach contradicts the inclusive message of Christianity and perpetuates social divisions.

DOING THE DEVIL'S WORK BEHIND THE CHRISTIAN MASK

Selective Compassion and Social Justice: Some Christian communities may prioritize specific social justice issues over others, neglecting or downplaying topics such as poverty, racism, or environmental degradation. This selective approach to compassion and justice undermines the holistic message of Christianity, which calls for love and care for all people and creation.

Selective Compassion in Humanitarian Aid: Some Christian humanitarian organizations may engage in selective compassion, providing aid or assistance only to those who share their religious beliefs or conform to specific moral standards. This selective approach can overlook the needs of marginalized or vulnerable populations and perpetuate inequalities in access to resources and support.

Selective Embrace of Christian Charity in Corporate Social Responsibility: Some corporations may selectively embrace Christian charity in their corporate social responsibility initiatives, focusing on philanthropy or community outreach while neglecting broader issues of social justice, labor rights, and environmental sustainability. This selective embrace can perpetuate corporate exploitation and harm communities and ecosystems.

Selective Embrace of Christian Charity in Corporate Social Responsibility: Some corporations may selectively embrace Christian charity in their corporate social responsibility initiatives, focusing on philanthropy or community outreach while neglecting broader issues of social justice, labor rights, and environmental sustainability. This selective embrace can perpetuate corporate exploitation and harm communities and ecosystems.

Selective Embrace of Christian Charity in Corporate Social Responsibility: Some corporations may selectively embrace Christian charity in their corporate social responsibility initiatives, focusing on philanthropy or community outreach while neglecting broader issues of social justice, labor rights, and environmental sustainability. This selective embrace can perpetuate corporate exploitation and harm communities and ecosystems.

Selective Embrace of Christian Charity in Foreign Aid: Some governments or international organizations may selectively embrace Christian charity in their foreign aid programs, assisting countries or populations perceived as morally deserving while neglecting others in need. This selective embrace can perpetuate disparities and inequalities in global development efforts.

Selective Embrace of Christian Humanitarianism: Some humanitarian organizations may selectively embrace Christian principles of compassion and service, focusing on charity or relief efforts while neglecting broader social justice issues, systemic change, and addressing root causes of poverty and inequality. This selective embrace can perpetuate cycles of dependence and hinder sustainable development.

Selective Embrace of Christian Morality in Corporate Governance: Corporations may selectively embrace Christian morality in their corporate governance practices, promoting values such as honesty, integrity, and accountability while neglecting broader issues of corporate responsibility, sustainability, and ethical leadership. This selective embrace can lead to ethical lapses and reputational damage for companies.

Selective Embrace of Christian Morality in Corporate Social Responsibility: Corporations may selectively embrace Christian morality in their corporate social responsibility initiatives, focusing on philanthropy or community outreach while neglecting broader issues of social justice, labor rights, and environmental sustainability. This selective embrace can perpetuate corporate exploitation and harm communities and ecosystems.

Selective Embrace of Christian Morality in International Relations: Some governments or international organizations may selectively apply Christian morality in their international relations, prioritizing strategic interests or geopolitical considerations over principles of peace, justice, and human rights. This selective application can lead to conflicts, injustices, and human rights abuses worldwide.

Selective Embrace of Christian Morality in International Relations: Some governments or international organizations may selectively apply Christian morality in their international relations, prioritizing strategic interests or geopolitical considerations over principles of peace, justice, and human rights. This selective application can lead to conflicts, injustices, and human rights abuses worldwide.

Selective Embrace of Religious Pluralism: Some Christians may selectively embrace religious pluralism, advocating for tolerance and understanding towards certain religious groups while excluding or marginalizing others. This selective embrace can reinforce religious hierarchies and hinder genuine dialogue and cooperation between faith traditions.

Selective Emphasis on Prosperity Theology: Some Christian communities may disproportionately emphasize prosperity theology, which equates material wealth and success with spiritual favor while neglecting teachings on social justice, compassion, and humility. This selective emphasis can distort the valid message of Christianity and perpetuate materialistic values.

Selective Interpretation of Christian Doctrine: Individuals or groups may selectively interpret Christian doctrine to justify their biases or prejudices, ignoring or downplaying teachings that challenge their worldview. This cherry-picking of scripture can lead to distorted beliefs and actions that are not in line with the inclusive and compassionate message of Christianity.

Selective Interpretation of Scripture to Justify Harmful Practices: Some individuals or groups may cherry-pick specific passages from religious texts to justify harmful practices or beliefs, such as misogyny, racism, or violence. By selectively interpreting scripture out of context or ignoring broader themes of love and compassion, they distort the message of Christianity and perpetuate harm in the name of religion.

Selective Invocation of Divine Providence: Some individuals or groups may invoke divine providence to justify their success or privilege while ignoring or downplaying the suffering or adversity others face. This selective invocation of divine favor can perpetuate myths of meritocracy and undermine empathy and solidarity with those less fortunate.

Selective Memory and Denial of Historical Atrocities: Some Christians may engage in selective memory or denial of historical atrocities committed in the name of Christianity, refusing to acknowledge or address past wrongs such as religious persecution, colonialism, or forced conversions. This denial can perpetuate historical injustices and hinder efforts toward reconciliation and healing.

Selective Memory in Christian Activism: In social or political activism, there may be a tendency to selectively remember or emphasize specific issues or causes while neglecting others, leading to inconsistencies in advocacy efforts. This selective memory can undermine the effectiveness of Christian witnesses and hinder progress toward social justice and systemic change.

Selective Memory in Historical Narratives: Christians may use selective memory or revisionist history, cherry-picking historical events or figures to fit a preferred narrative of Christian triumphalism or persecution. This selective approach to history can perpetuate myths and distortions that hinder honest reflection and reconciliation.

Selective Memory in Personal Testimonies: Individuals sharing personal testimonies of their faith journey may selectively emphasize or omit specific details to fit a narrative of triumph or redemption, downplaying struggles, doubts, or failures. This selective memory can create unrealistic expectations and hinder genuine dialogue about the complexities of faith.

Selective Memory of Church History: Christians may selectively remember or interpret historical events to fit a preferred narrative of their faith's past, ignoring or downplaying episodes of violence, corruption, or oppression perpetrated by the church. This whitewashing of history hinders honest reflection and reconciliation with past wrongs.

Selective Representation of Christian Diversity in Media: Media representations of Christianity may selectively focus on certain denominations or interpretations of the faith while neglecting others, leading to stereotypes and misconceptions about the diversity of Christian beliefs and practices. This selective representation can hinder understanding and dialogue between different Christian traditions.

Selective Social Engagement: While Christianity emphasizes love and compassion for all people, some Christians may engage in selective social activism, prioritizing specific issues while neglecting others. This selective engagement can reflect underlying biases or prejudices and perpetuate societal systemic injustices.

Televangelists Engaged in Financial Scandals: Some prominent televangelists have been embroiled in financial scandals, where they misused donations meant for charitable or religious purposes for personal gain. Examples include Jim Bakker and his PTL Club, which collapsed amid accusations of accounting fraud and mismanagement, and televangelist Benny Hinn, who faced scrutiny over his lavish lifestyle and alleged misuse of funds.

Weaponization of Religious Guilt: Some religious leaders or organizations may use guilt as a tool for control or manipulation, instilling fear or shame in followers to compel obedience or compliance with certain beliefs or practices. This manipulation can have damaging effects on individuals' mental and emotional well-being and undermine their sense of autonomy and agency.

Weaponization of Religious Language for Political Ends: Politicians or political movements may use religious language and imagery to rally support for their policies or agendas, even if those policies do not align with Christian values. This manipulation of religious sentiment for political gain can lead to polarization and division within society, undermining the true spirit of Christianity.

While these examples highlight instances where individuals have betrayed the principles of Christianity, it's essential to recognize that they do not represent the entirety of the Christian faith. Christianity teaches love, compassion, forgiveness, and humility at its core. When individuals deviate from these principles and engage in actions that harm others or contradict Christian teachings, they do not truly embody their faith's values. Christians need to hold themselves and their leaders accountable, strive for integrity and authenticity, and work towards building a more just and compassionate world.

Ask Yourself, What Of The Above Are You Doing And Why?

Asking oneself what aspects of faithfulness or hypocrisy they may be exhibiting and why prompts deep introspection into one's beliefs, actions, and motivations. Here's a breakdown of how to approach this question:

Self-Reflection on Actions: Take inventory of your recent actions and behaviors. Are there instances where you have acted following your professed beliefs and values, demonstrating faithfulness in your conduct? Conversely, are there times when you have fallen short of living up to your ideals, perhaps exhibiting hypocrisy?

Identifying Motivations: Probe more deeply into the motivations behind your actions. When you align with your beliefs, what drives you to do so? Is it a genuine commitment to your principles, a desire to uphold moral integrity, or a sense of duty to your faith? On the other hand, when you behave hypocritically, what underlying factors may be at play? Are internal conflicts, external pressures, or personal weaknesses contributing to this inconsistency?

Exploring Intentions: Reflect on the intentions behind your actions. Are you consciously striving to live a life of integrity and authenticity, guided by your core values and beliefs? Or are there times when you may prioritize self-interest, societal approval, or convenience over ethical considerations, leading to actions that contradict your professed convictions?

Assessing Impact: Consider the impact of your actions on yourself and others. How does acting faithfully contribute to your sense of fulfillment, purpose, and well-being? Conversely, what consequences does it have for your relationships, reputation, and inner peace when you engage in hypocritical behavior?

Seeking Alignment: Strive to align your beliefs, intentions, and actions closely. Are there areas where you can bridge the gap between what you profess to believe and how you behave? How can you cultivate greater integrity, consistency, and authenticity in your thoughts, words, and deeds?

By asking oneself what aspects of faithfulness or hypocrisy we may be exhibiting and why - individuals can gain valuable insights into their moral character, motivations, and inner workings. This introspective inquiry lays the groundwork for personal growth, ethical refinement, and cultivating a more harmonious and meaningful life.

Don't miss out!

Visit the website below and you can sign up to receive emails whenever Ydna Serdna publishes a new book. There's no charge and no obligation.

https://books2read.com/r/B-A-LVZQB-DLSOD

About the Author

Ydna Serdna is a devout Christian and has always questioned religion, especially why it is contradictory and why people have weaponizcd it. He lives in Santa Monica, California, with his family. His hobbies include theology, bible studies, and learning about other religions.

Read more at https://www.behindthechristianmask.com/.

About the Publisher

Writers Sidekick Publishing was established in 2021. To publish its Writers Sidekick Notebook Series. Notebooks that help guide writers to organize and keep track of their characters, settings, plot, and more.

Read more at www.writerssidekick.com.